COMMUNICATION SYSTEMS AND COMPUTER NETWORKS

ELLIS HORWOOD SERIES IN
ELECTRICAL AND ELECTRONIC ENGINEERING

Series Editor: PETER BRANDON,
Emeritus Professor of Electrical and Electronic Engineering, University of Cambridge

ELECTRONIC AND COMMUNICATION ENGINEERING

COMMUNICATION SYSTEMS AND COMPUTER NETWORKS

R. L. BREWSTER, H.N.C., M.Sc., Ph.D.
Department of Electrical and Electronic Engineering
and Applied Physics
Aston University, Birmingham

ELLIS HORWOOD LIMITED
Publishers · Chichester

Halsted Press: a division of
JOHN WILEY & SONS
New York · Chichester · Brisbane · Toronto

First published in 1989 by
ELLIS HORWOOD LIMITED
Market Cross House, Cooper Street,
Chichester, West Sussex, PO19 1EB, England
The publisher's colophon is reproduced from James Gillison's drawing of the ancient Market Cross, Chichester.

Distributors:

Australia and New Zealand:
JACARANDA WILEY LIMITED
GPO Box 859, Brisbane, Queensland 4001, Australia

Canada:
JOHN WILEY & SONS CANADA LIMITED
22 Worcester Road, Rexdale, Ontario, Canada

Europe and Africa:
JOHN WILEY & SONS LIMITED
Baffins Lane, Chichester, West Sussex, England

North and South America and the rest of the world:
Halsted Press: a division of
JOHN WILEY & SONS
605 Third Avenue, New York, NY 10158, USA

South-East Asia
JOHN WILEY & SONS (SEA) PTE LIMITED
37 Jalan Pemimpin # 05–04
Block B, Union Industrial Building, Singapore 2057

Indian Subcontinent
WILEY EASTERN LIMITED
4835/24 Ansari Road
Daryaganj, New Delhi 110002, India

© **1989 R.L. Brewster/Ellis Horwood Limited**

British Library Cataloguing in Publication Data
Brewster, R.L. (Ronald L.), *1932–*
Communication systems and computer networks
1. Computer systems. Communications networks
I. Title
004.6

Library of Congress data available

ISBN 0–7458–0552–3 (Ellis Horwood Limited — Library Edn.)
ISBN 0–7458–0745–3 (Ellis Horwood Limited — Student Edn.)
ISBN 0–470–21489–9 (Halsted Press)

Printed in Great Britain by Hartnolls, Bodmin

Table of Contents

Preface

Over the last two decades the telecommunications network has moved from being almost exclusively used for telephony to becoming a fully integrated services digital network. My previous book "Telecommunications Technology" was addressed mainly to those who are, or will be, employed in the business of providing telecommunications facilities to the ever-widening variety of users. This book is written with a rather different emphasis. It is intended mainly for the growing number of users of the network for the purposes of digital communication. Many, if not most of these, are involved one way or another, in the use of computers as part of a data communications network.

Some of the material in this book will also be found in the previous book. In many cases it has been expanded to embrace in more detail the specifically computer-oriented aspects of interfacing with the telecommunications infrastructure and to introduce some new facilities that have come into being since the previous book was written. In other places the text has been edited to remove some of the mathematical concepts that would be appropriate to the network designer but are only likely to be a distraction to the network user.

The book has been prepared from notes of lectures given as a course in Communication Systems and Computer Networks which forms part of the M.Sc. programme in Information Technology at Aston University. This is a conversion programme for graduates from a variety of disciplines, many non-technical, who have decided to pursue a new career in a rapidly expanding and exciting area of modern technological innovation. As with the previous book, the notes have been gathered from many sources and frequently updated over a number of years. The origins of much of the information are therefore no longer known and it would be impossible to cite references in any acceptable way. I have, therefore, rather included a bibliography at the end of the book which includes those books I have on my shelf which have been an inspiration to me over the years I have taught the course, those books I have from time to time included in the recommended reading lists, and those books and papers I regard as classic works on specific topics and to which I turn for more specialised information. I hope the reader will find the list useful.

Thanks are due to my many colleagues who have passed on to me from time to time, in lectures, conferences and in private discussion, much of the material on which my present lecture course is based. Their influence will no doubt be apparent in some places in the book, although I have avoided, as far as possible, direct reproduction of their source material. It is just possible that a colleague may happen to recognise a diagram here or there that bears some marked similarity to his own original. If so, I hope he will forgive me and take it as a complement to his own clarity of presentation that I was unable to better his original contribution.

Finally my special thanks to Mrs. Brenda Phillips, who patiently implemented numerous changes in format in order to produce the final manuscript in camera-ready form.

Birmingham, March 1989   R.L.Brewster

1
Background and basics.

INTRODUCTION

Data is the very essence of computing; every computer operation involves the manipulation of data in some form or another. To carry out meaningful operations, the computer has first to be supplied with the appropriate data. Data can be fed into the computer in a number of ways. Familiar methods are through keyboards, card and tape readers, disk drives and optical character readers. Other more specialist devices also exist, such as measurement transducers and proximity sensors.

It is pointless manipulating data in a computer if it is not subsequently to be made available for further use. Typical data output devices are visual display units, printers, control transducers and alarms. Processed data may also be stored on cards, tape or disk so that it can be used again at a later date. In large computer networks data is often exchanged directly between computers within the network. The efficient transmission of data to and from data terminal equipment, sometimes referred to as computer peripherals, and between computers themselves, is therefore a vitally important function.

When computers first came into general use in the early 1950's they were self-contained units with terminals which were either integral with the processor or were installed adjacent to the main equipment. There was thus no problem of interconnection; the units were simply connected together using multi-core cable with sufficient wires of adequate quality to carry separately all the necessary data and control signals. Very quickly, however, it became desirable to separate the terminal from the central processor at distances where it was no longer economical to use multicore cables. Instead, a cable consisting of a single wire pair was used and techniques for combining the data and control signals into a single data stream were devised.

The next development was the need to operate from terminals from remote locations, requiring the transmission of data over lines passing outside the site at which the computer mainframe was situated. This need arose through the growth of centralised control systems, such as those operated by Gas Boards and Water Authorities, and the demand for Computer Bureau facilities.

At the same time, in the U.K., all communication facilities outside the private site were still the sole prerogative of British Telecom (then the Post Office). The provision of data transmission facilities offered a new challenge; until this time the vast majority of communication traffic had been telephony, though for many years a relatively small amount of telegraphy had also been carried. Because of its ready availability, it was obviously desirable to use, if at all possible, the public telephone network to carry the new data traffic from remote terminals to the centralised computer facility. The lines, however, had not been designed with digital signals in mind, and their characteristics thus appeared to be inappropriate for this application. In order to match the digital signals to the line characteristics, MODEMS were developed to interface the digital equipment to the telephone network. These modems were provided by the Post Office as part of the data transmission facility offered under the commercial name of DATEL services.

Because of limitations set by noise and channel bandwidth, the maximum data rate obtainable over the public switched telephone network is about 2.4 kbits/s, although rates of 4.8 kbits/s, or even 9.6 kbits/s, are available over special-quality private leased telephone circuits. For long distance trunk data services it was possible to lease a 'group-band' circuit, capable of 48 kbits/s transmission. This, however, occupied a bandwidth equivalent to 12 telephone circuits.

More recently, it has become common practice to transmit speech signals in the junction and trunk telephone network using pulse-code-modulation (p.c.m.). In p.c.m. the speech signal is sampled and quantised and converted into a digital signal at a transmission-rate of 64 kbits/s. This facility may be utilised for the transmission of data, the service being offered in the U.K. by British Telecom under the title KILOSTREAM. In this way, a data rate of 64 kbits/s can be achieved over the equivalent of one single telephone speech circuit. Alternatively, the equivalent of 30 p.c.m. speech channels can be used as a single data transmission facility operating at 2.04 Mbits/s., the service being offered under the title

MEGASTREAM. With the growth of the digital speech network and the introduction of digital switching techniques (System X), it is planned that in the not-to-distant future an 'Integrated Services Digital Network' (ISDN) will be provided which will carry both data and digitally-encoded speech signals without discrimination. The emergence of such a service will ultimately make the DATEL services, together with their expensive modems, increasingly obsolete.

The concept of the DATEL services is to provide a 'transparent' data transmission facility such that the provider of the carrier service has no interest in either the format or the significance of the transmitted data stream. In order to allow terminals to be readily connected together via the network, a standard equipment interface was established by CCITT. This interface is widely known as the V24 interface. A similar (though not identical) interface is in use in the USA and is known as the RS232 interface. The interface not only facilitates the actual transfer of data between the data terminal equipment (DTE) and the line terminating equpment (LTE), but also provides certain control signals which allow some interaction between the terminal and the network.

With the advance of computer technology and the widespread introduction of the microprocessor, terminal equipment has become more sophisticated and distributed computing power has become commonplace. Data networks have therefore been set up to allow computers and data terminals to communicate together as required by the user. Most networks of this type are set up within the confines of a factory site, university campus or office block. These networks do not, therefore, make use of public network transmission facilities. They operate on wideband circuits, data being multiplexed and assigned using a suitable network protocol. Such networks are known as 'Local Area Networks' or LANs.

Many large organisations now operate data networks on a regional, national, or even international basis. In countries, such as the USA, where the PTT have not had a monopoly of telecommunication transmission, independent data networks have developed, both for private and public data service. In the UK, where, until recently, British Telecom have had a monopoly on telecommunication transmission, the structure of wide area data networks has been strongly influenced by the data services available from British Telecom. This has normally meant either interconnecting local data centres using the DATEL services or digital circuits

primarily intended for p.c.m. (KILOSTREAM and MEGASTREAM); although
B.T. have also been progressively developing a packet-switched data network.

The development of data networks has led to the concept of Open Systems
Interconnection (OSI).   The purpose of OSI is to enable a wide variety of data
terminals from different manufacturers to be interconnected freely over common
data transmission facilities.   This has meant the development of specifications and
network protocols which enable such operation to take place.   These specifications
are based on a 7-layer protocol structure proposed by the International Standards
Organisation (ISO) and known as the ISO reference model for OSI.   The structure
and significance of this model is discussed in a later chapter.

BACK TO BASICS

Information within a computer is normally represented by binary symbols which
are manipulated as series of electrical impulses.   A single binary symbol is

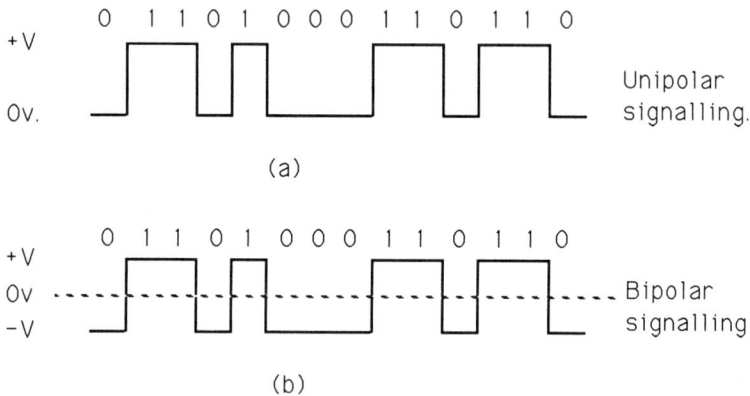

Fig.1.1 - Serial binary data signals.

represented by a single electrical impulse.   The two binary states 0 and 1 can be
represented either by the presence or absence of a pulse, or by pulses of opposite
polarity. A serial stream of binary data symbols thus consists of an electrical
signal composed of alternations between two voltage amplitudes.   Where the binary
symbol is represented by the presence or absence of a pulse, the electrical signal

alternates between a voltage V and zero volts a shown in Fig.1.1(a).   Since the signal is always of the same polarity the signalling is known as unipolar.   Where the binary symbols are represented by pulses of opposite polarity, the electrical signal alternates between positive and negative voltage amplitudes +V and -V as shown in Fig.1.1(b).   Since the signal can be of either polarity the signalling is known as bipolar.   We shall now look at the effect that transmission over a practical communication channel has on the shape of the electrical signal.   Firstly we shall begin by considering the effect on a single pulse transmitted in isolation.   Because electrical signals obey the law of superposition, that is, the effect on each pulse forming part of the complete signal is additive, then we can extrapolate from the single pulse to the electrical signal representing a string of binary symbols.

Any electrical signal can be broken down into a set of 'frequency components' by a mathematical process known as Fourier analysis.   Each component consists of a periodic sinusoidal waveform, the frequency being defined as the number of periods, or cycles, in unit time.   If the unit of time is 1 second, then the frequency is measured in Hertz (Hz).   The collection of frequency components for a specific signal is referred to as its spectral content or, simply, its spectrum.   In any practical transmission channel, some frequency components are transmitted more readily than others.   A channel that passes the lower frequencies without attenuation but removes the higher frequency components is known as a low-pass channel.   One which passes the higher frequencies but attenuates the low frequencies is known as a high-pass channel.   One that passes a range of frequencies but attenuates both the higher and lower frequencies is known as a band-pass channel.   Conversely, a band-stop channel will transmit all frequencies except for a band of frequencies somewhere in the range of frequencies under consideration. Generally we shall be concerned only with low-pass and band-pass channels since most practical channels fall into one or other of these categories.

A connection established using wire conductors will normally be a low-pass channel.   When we transmit our signal over such a channel, the high frequency components of the signal are removed.   This leads to a rounding of the received pulse as shown in Figs.1.2(a) and (b).   If the transition from the pass-band, where the frequency components are transmitted virtually unattenuated, to the stop-band, where the frequency components are heavily attenuated, is abrupt, then   some

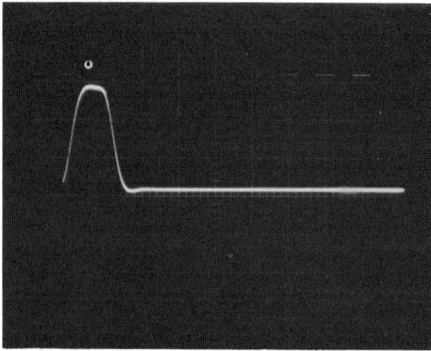

(a) f_c = 30KHz., r_c = 6 dB/Octave.

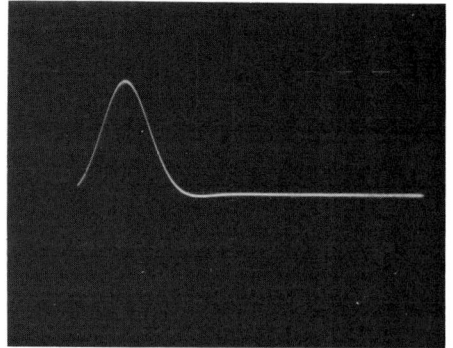

(b) f_c = 10KHz., r_c = 6 dB/Octave.

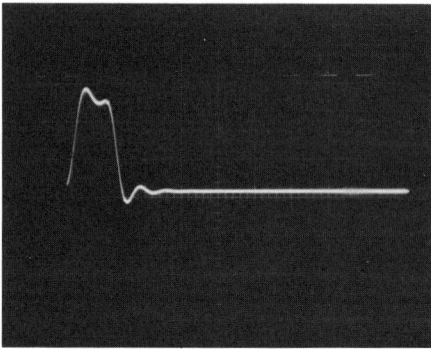

(c) f_c = 30KHz., r_c =12 dB/Octave.

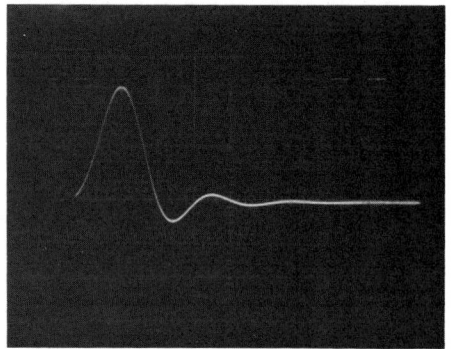

(d) f_c = 10KHz., r_c =12 dB/Octave.

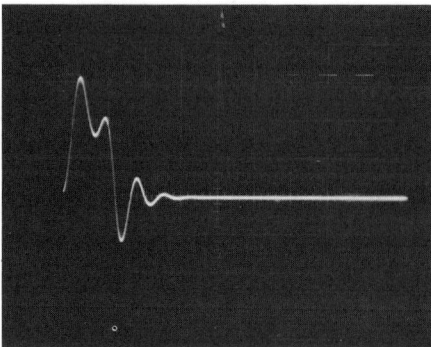

(e) f_c = 30KHz., r_c =18 dB/Octave.

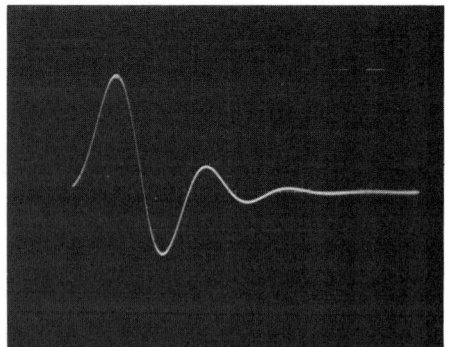

(f) f_c = 10KHz., r_c =18 dB/Octave.

Fig.1.2 - Impulse responses of low-pass channel.

f_c = cut-off frequency, r_c = cut-off rate.

Transmitted pulse width = 50µS (1 square)

oscillation also occurs at the edges of the pulse. This is shown in Figs.1.2(c) to (f). The frequency of the oscillation depends on the cut-off frequency and the amplitude of the oscillation depends on the abruptness of the cut-off. It is evident from the oscillograms given in Fig.1.2 that generally the pulses become more dispersed in time as the bandwidth (i.e. the cut-off frequency) of the channel is reduced. In a sequence of pulses representing a string of binary digits it is clear that pulses will be stretched so that they overlap into the time period occupied by adjacent pulses. This gives rise to what is known as "intersymbol interference". Clearly this can give rise to erroneous interpretation of the received data sequence.

As far back as 1928, Nyquist demonstrated that it is possible, at least in principle, to transmit pulses through a network, without intersymbol interference, at a rate not exceeding twice the channel bandwidth. In order to achieve this rate, it is necessary that the channel has certain specific features associated with its transmission characteristics. To obtain these features in practice, it is usual to incorporate additional circuit elements in the transmission path known as "channel shaping filters". Before we can decide on the nature of these filters, it will be necessary for us to look in a little more detail at the effect of the channel transmisson characteristics on the shape of the data pulse.

THE EFFECT OF THE CHANNEL ON THE DATA PULSE

We have seen that when a data pulse is transmitted through a communication channel it is inevitably distorted because of band-limiting and other non-ideal features in the transmission characteristics. It is usual to define the transmitted and received pulses as functions of time, whereas it is usual to define the channel characteristics as functions of frequency. To calculate the effect of the channel characteristics on the pulse response we therefore have to make use of the Fourier transform. The Fourier transform is a mathematical relationship that enables us to determine the time response from the frequency characteristics of signals and of networks such as transmission channels and filters. The reverse operation is mathematically similar and is known as the inverse Fourier transform. If you are not mathematically inclined you need not worry at this stage, as we shall not actually be carrying out any calculations using the Fourier transform. It is introduced here simply to let you know what tools are available to arrive at the results given in the following sections.

There are two ways of using Fourier transforms to determine the effect of the channel on the pulse shape.   These are illustrated in Fig 1.3.   Firstly, we could determine the spectral content of the input pulse $X(\omega)$. By multiplying this with the channel characteristic $G(\omega)$ we obtain the spectral content of the output pulse $Y(\omega)$, which we can now transform back into the time response y(t).   An alternative approach is to   determine   the   inverse   Fourier   transform   of   the   channel

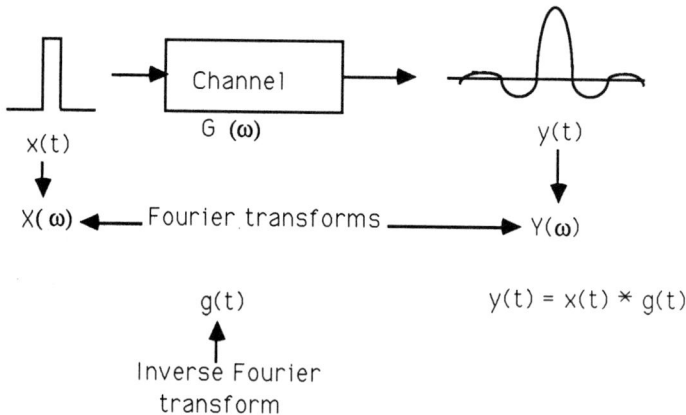

Fig.1.3 - Use of Fourier transform to determine network response.

The asterisk denotes convolution, i.e. $y(t) = \int_{-\infty}^{\infty} x(\tau).g(t-\tau)d\tau$

characteristic g(t) and to convolve this with the input pulse x(t). This will yield the output pulse response y(t) directly.   The inverse Fourier transform g(t) of the channel characteristic $G(\omega)$ is in fact the channel impulse response, that is the output that would be obtained if the input to the channel were a 'dirac' impulse d(t). This is illustrated in Fig 1.4.

The dirac impulse consists of an idealised pulse of infinite amplitude and infinitesimal time duration and having an 'area' of unity.   It is, of course, impossible to generate such an impulse in practice, but it is a convenient

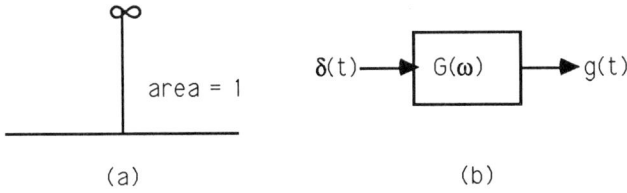

Fig. 1.4 - Definition of impulse response.

(a) Dirac impulse δ (t),   (b) Impulse response g(t).

mathematical concept for analysis of this kind. It should be noted that a network is uniquely defined by its impulse response in exactly the same way as it is defined by its amplitude and phase-versus-frequency characteristics.

EFFECT OF BAND-LIMITING ON A DIRAC IMPULSE

If a channel has ideal characteristics except that frequencies beyond some 'cut-off' frequency are completely attenuated, the response of such a channel to an impulse is the familiar sin x/x form:

$$g(t) = \frac{\sin 2\pi Wt}{2\pi Wt}$$

Thus if a pulse which is short enough to be considered an impulse is applied to the input of an ideal band-limited channel, the waveform at the channel output is a sin X/X waveform with oscillating tails as shown in Fig.1.5.

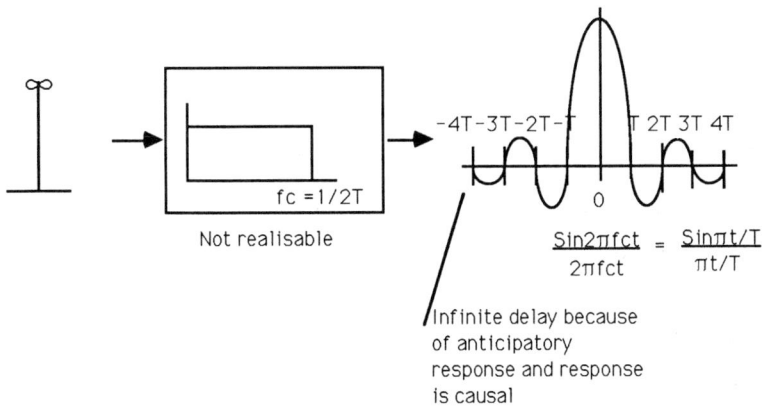

Fig.1.5 - Impulse response of ideal band-limited channel.

If we just wanted to transmit a single pulse, there would be no problem, but when we transmit a succession of pulses, the tails caused by previous pulses may obscure the main response due to the pulse of the present instant. This is termed 'intersymbol interference'. The effect of intersymbol interference can be completely eliminated in the ideal band-limited channel by sending pulses with a pulse spacing of $T = 1/2W$. That is, if the cut-off frequency of the channel is W Hz, we send 2W pulses per second. This is because g(t), the channel impulse response, is zero at $\pm 1/2W$, $\pm 2/2W$, $\pm 3/2W$, etc. Thus, at $t = nT$, the channel output is solely the main lobe of the response of the channel to the nth pulse; the response of the channel to all other input pulses is zero at this instant, as shown in Fig.1.6. Provided, therefore, the signal is sampled at the appropriate instant, it is possible to observe the relevant symbol without interference.

In practice it is difficult to construct band-limiting filters giving a good approximation to the sin x/x impulse response and, in any case, a system using the sin x/x response would be sensitive to small timing errors. What is needed is a channel whose response has the same property as the sin x/x function in that it is zero at $t = \pm T$, $\pm 2T$, etc. but which has a gentler roll-off with increasing frequency. Nyquist showed that if the channel gain characteristic has 'vestigial' symmetry about a frequency equal to half the pulse transmission rate, and has a linear phase characteristic, then the impulse response of the channel has nulls at the appropriate points. Vestigial symmetry implies odd symmetry but offset in amplitude so that

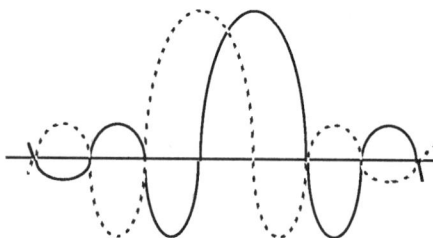

Fig.1.6 - Channel response with zero intersymbol interference at sampling instants.

the characteristic subsequently falls to zero value rather than ranging between equal positive and negative amplitude values. A suitable response which can be closely

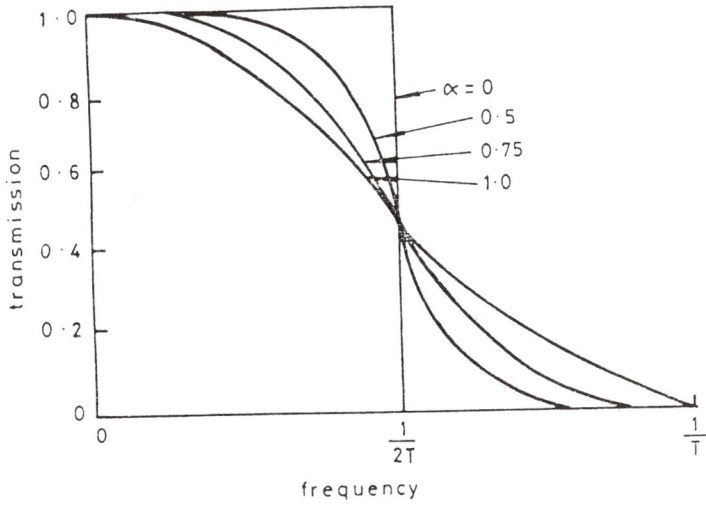

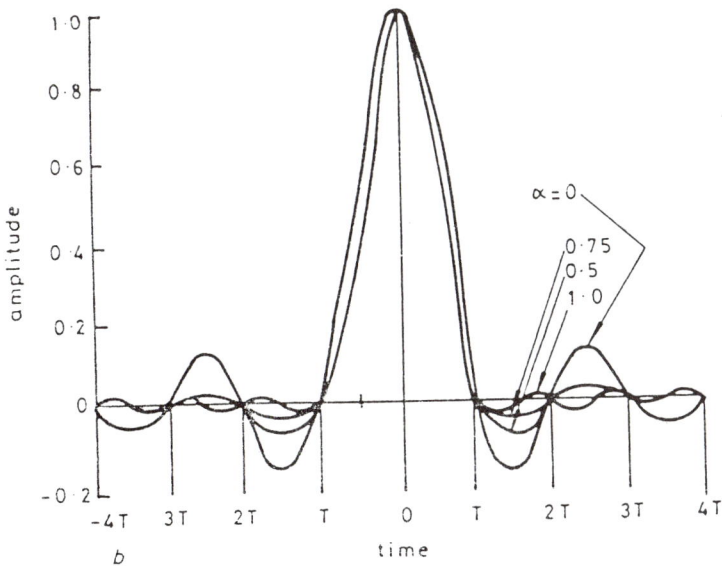

Fig.1.7 - The raised cosine filter characteristics. (a) Raised-cosine roll-off characteristics.
(b) Impulse responses of r.c.r.o. characteristics.

approximated to in practice is that known as the 'raised cosine roll-off' characteristic.   This is illustrated in Fig.1.7(a).   The impulse responses corresponding to various roll-off factors are shown in Fig.1.7(b).   It will be seen that the oscillations in the pulse tails decreases as the excess bandwidth is increased. This means that the sampling becomes less critical in signal detection as the roll-off factor is increased.

MODIFICATION OF CHANNEL CHARACTERISTIC FOR FINITE DURATION PULSES

In practice we shall not normally be transmitting impulses, but finite duration pulses of time duration T_1.   If we take a train of pulses of finite duration T_1 repeated at intervals of time T_2 as shown in Fig.1.8(a), then, by Fourier analysis, we obtain the spectrum of the pulse train as illustrated in Fig.1.8(b).   The spectrum consists of lines spaced at frequency intervals of $1/T_2$ Hz,   the spectrum envelope following

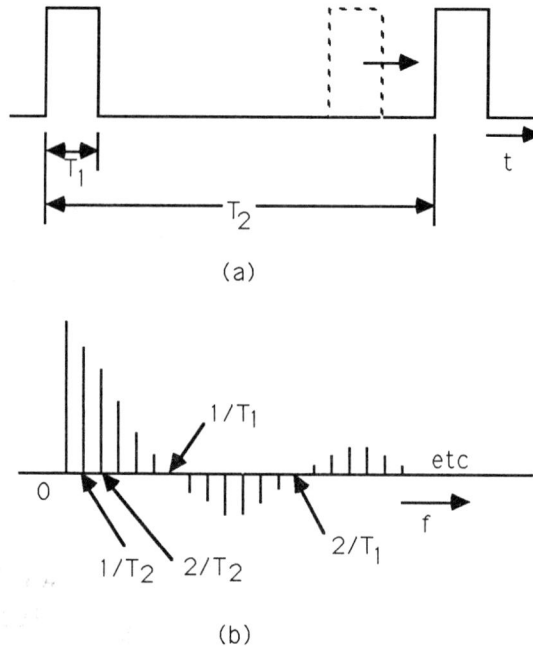

(a)

(b)

Fig.1.8 - Pulse spectrum. (a) Repetitive pulse waveform. (b) Repetitive pulse spectrum.

the sin x/x shape, with the zeros in the sin x/x function occuring at frequencies n/T_1

Hz, where $n = \pm1, \pm2, \pm3$, etc.   Clearly, as the interval between the pulses is

increased, the spectrum lines close up and in the limit, when the second pulse goes to

infinity and we are left with one single pulse, the spectrum becomes continuous with

a sin x/x envelope.   Similarly, if the pulse duration is reduced, the zeros in the sin

x/x envelope move apart and in the limit, when the pulse becomes a dirac impulse,

the first zero moves out to infinity and the spectrum becomes flat over any finite

range.   Thus the spectrum of a single dirac impulse is continuous and flat over the

whole frequency range.   The desired channel response to a finite duration pulse is

the same as the impulse response obtained when the vestigial symmetry of the

channel occurs about a frequency 1/2T.   To achieve this, we need to modify the

channel characteristic to allow for the sin x/x spectrum shape of the finite duration

pulse.   The concept is illistrated in Fig.1.9.   Since the spectrum for the impulse is

flat, $F(\omega)$ will be the inverse of the spectrum $X(\omega)$ for the pulse x(t), i.e.

$$F(\omega) = \frac{1}{X(\omega)}$$

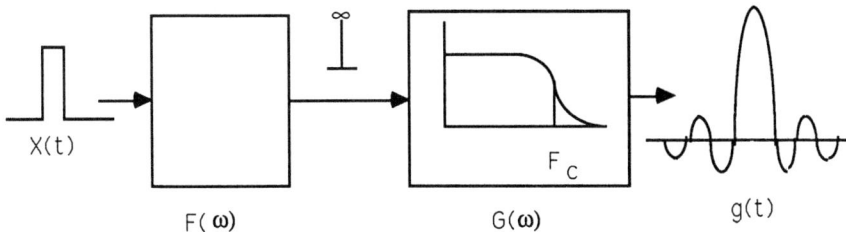

Fig.1.9 - Allowance for finite duration pulse.

Thus, if we wish to obtain g(t) from x(t), we need to pass the signal through a

channel with a gain-frequency response

$$Y(\omega) = \frac{1}{x(\omega)} \times G(\omega).$$

Since $G(\omega) = 0$ for $f \geq f_c + f_r$, we need not define $X(\omega)$ outside this range. In this way we can determine the channel response required to give zero intersymbol interference at sampling instants spaced at intervals of T time units apart for data represented by finite-width pulses of duration T. The process is illustrated in Fig.1.10.

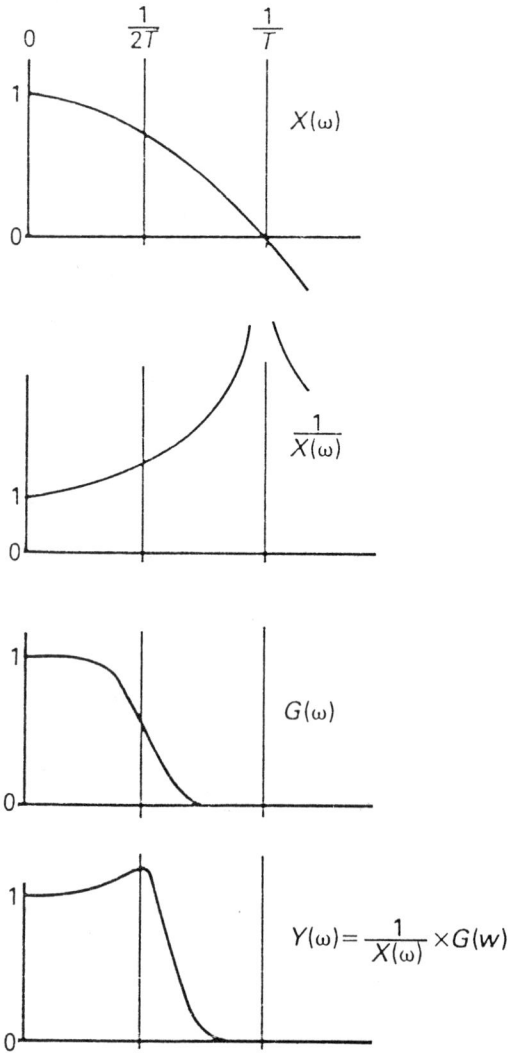

Fig.1.10 - Ideal channel response for finite duration pulse.

The desired channel rsponse is obtained in practice by the use of 'channel shaping filters' which form part of the channel terminating equipment. The channel bandwidth is chosen so that in the pass-band region the effect of the shaping filter predominates over any frequency-dependent attenuation that may occur in the transmission medium. This means that a larger bandwidth can be utilised if a smaller roll-off factor is used. However, this will be associated with more critical timing in the sampling process for signal detection. The usual practice is to divide the overall channel shaping requirement between two identical filters, one at the transmitting terminal and the other at the receive terminal. In this way the channel signal-to-noise ratio is optimised at the same time as providing the required channel impulse response.

EYE PATTERNS

The eye pattern is a convenient method of displaying on an oscilloscope the effect of noise and intersymbol interference on a received data signal. The received signal voltage is used to deflect the oscilloscope trace vertically and the horizontal sweep is synchronised to the data symbol rate. The resulting display for a random bipolar binary data sequence is shown in Fig.1.11(a). The reason for the name 'eye pattern' is apparent. The eye pattern for a four-level random data sequence is shown in Fig.1.11(b). The optimum sampling instant to ensure correct decoding is where the 'eye' is widest open. In the absence of intersymbol interference and noise, all similar symbol amplitudes will pass through the same point at the optimum sampling instant. The effect of the tails in the response of adjacent symbols becomes significant away from this point and the noise margin before the onset of errrors is therefore significantly reduced if the signal in not optimally sampled. The eye pattern is extremely useful for making practical assessments of the effect of intersymbol interference in working data transmission systems.

EQUALISATION

Any imperfections in the transmission channel characteristics will inevitably lead to departures from the ideal channel impulse rsponse we have endeavoured to obtain for our channel by careful design of the channel shaping filters. Instead of passing through zero at intervals of time T, the impulse response takes on values as shown in Fig.1.12. There will thus be some intersymbol interference if consecutive data

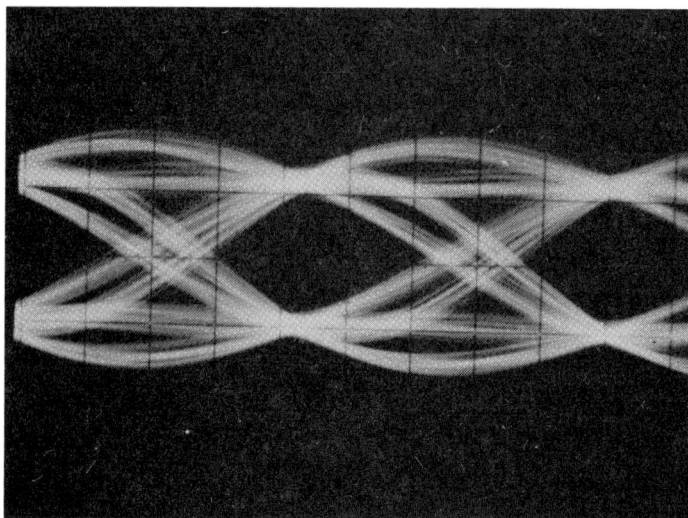

(a)

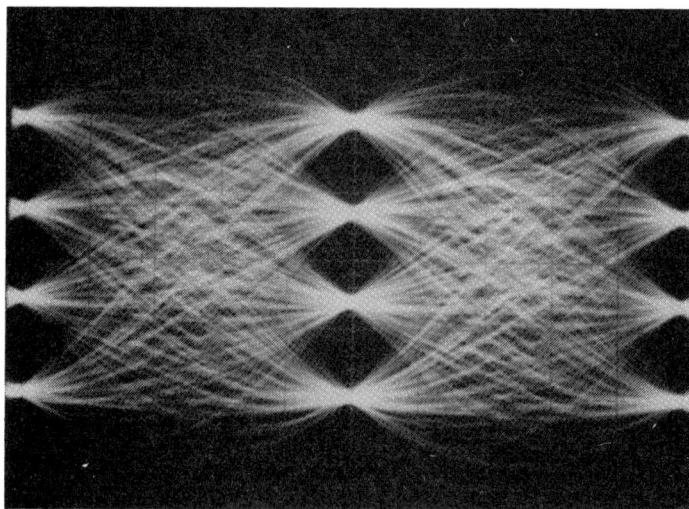

(b)

Fig.1.11 - Eye patterns. (a) Binary eye pattern. (b) Four-level eye pattern.

pulses are transmitted at intervals of time T. The magnitude of the resulting intersymbol interference largely depends on the degree to which the transmission conditions of the transmission medium depart from the ideal in the frequency band spanned by the pass-band of the shaping filter characteristics.

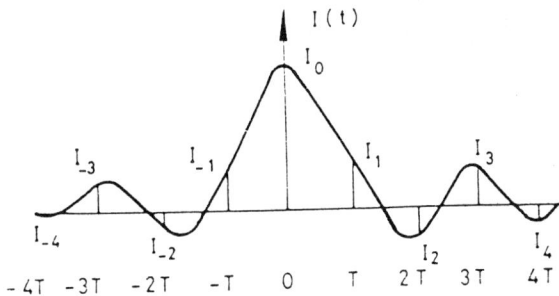

Fig.1.12 - Impulse response having intersymbol interference components

In a binary bipolar transmission system, a worst-case sequence could cause a total contribution to the intersymbol interference affecting a particular binary symbol of a magnitude equal to the sum of the magnitudes of the individual interfering samples. That is:

$$\text{Maximum possible intersymbol interference} = \sum_{\substack{n=-j \\ n\neq 0}}^{k} I_n$$

where -j to k is the range of samples over which the channel response I_n has significant (non-zero) values.

Normalising the sample amplitudes to that of the main sample gives a measure of intersymbol interference distortion (D), such that

$$D = \frac{1}{I_0} \sum_{\substack{n=-j \\ n\neq 0}}^{k} I_n$$

Referring back to our binary eye pattern given in Fig.1.11(a), it can be seen that, as the intersymbol interference increases, there will be a widening of the band formed where the two binary signalling levels would be optimally sampled. Thus we will observe an 'eye closure' effect. The effect of eye closure is to reduce the noise margin before the onset of errors. Eye closure is therefore associated with an increased error-rate in signal detection. If the eye becomes completely closed, then it becomes virtually impossible to carry out satisfactory detection by simply slicing the signal about the zero level. Complete closure of the binary eye occurs when $D \geq 1$.

The intersymbol interference can be reduced by the use of a transversal equaliser. The basic transversal equaliser consists of a delay-line tapped at intervals of time T. Each tap has associated with it a variable gain coefficient as shown in Fig.1.13.

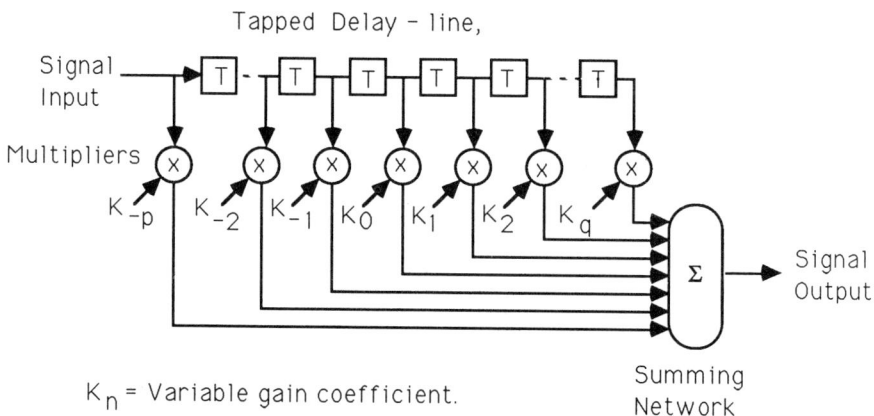

Fig.1.13 - Basic transversal equaliser.

The outputs from the coefficient multipliers are added together in a summing network to provide the equalised output. By suitable choice of the gain coefficients it is possible to reduce the intersymbol interference present in the channel. The sampled impulse response h(nT) (which we will henceforth write as h_n for simplicity) of the equaliser will be given by the values of the gain coefficients, that is

$$h_n = K_n, \quad -p \leq n \leq q, \text{ otherwise } h_n = 0.$$

If the impulse response of the channel is I_n, as shown in Fig.1.12, and has significant values only in the range $-j \leq n \leq k$, then the overall impulse response of the channel plus the equaliser will be

$$y_n = \sum_{x=-p}^{q} I_{(n-x)} K_x$$

This mathematical process is referred to as 'discrete convolution'. Thus y_n is formed by the discrete convolution of I_n with K_n, sometimes written as $y_n = I_n * K_n$.

Let us take as a practical example the case where $j = k = p = q = 2$. Then we can write the values of y_n as follows:

$$
\begin{aligned}
y_{-4} &= I_{-2}K_{-2} \\
y_{-3} &= I_{-1}K_{-2} + I_{-2}K_{-1} \\
y_{-2} &= I_0 \, K_{-2} + I_{-1}K_{-1} \; + I_{-2}K_0 && = 0 \\
y_{-1} &= I_1 \, K_{-2} + I_0 \, K_{-1} \; + I_{-1}K_0 + I_{-2}K_1 && = 0 \\
y_0 \; &= I_2 \, K_{-2} + I_1 \, K_{-1} \; + I_0 K_0 + I_{-1}K_1 \; + I_{-2}K_2 && = 1 \\
y_1 \; &= \qquad\quad I_2 \, K_{-1} \; + I_1 K_0 + I_0 \, K_1 \; + I_{-1}K_2 && = 0 \\
y_2 \; &= \qquad\qquad\qquad\quad I_2 K_0 \qquad + I_1 \, K_1 + I_0 \, K_2 && = 0 \\
y_3 \; &= \qquad\qquad\qquad\qquad\qquad I_2 \, K_1 \qquad\quad + I_1 \, K_2 \\
y_4 \; &= \qquad\qquad\qquad\qquad\qquad\qquad\quad I_2 \, K_2
\end{aligned}
$$

Note that y_n will have significant values over the range $-(j+p)$ to $(k+q)$, that is, the 'equalised' response is dispersed over a wider time span than the unequalised channel impulse response. However, we are able to adjust the coefficients of the equaliser so that $p+q+1$ samples in the equalised response have pre-determined values. One possible choice is to make $y_n = 0$, $-p \leq n \leq q$, $n \neq 0$ and $y_0 = 1$. This is known as zero-forcing.

Assuming that I_0 is significantly larger than any of the other values of I_n, then an examination of the table above will show that coefficient K_n is mainly effective in cancelling the intersymbol interference associated with the impulse response sample I_n. It can also be seen that the dispersed intersymbol interference samples remaining after equalisation result from the product of two small quantities and are therefore generally small compared to the intersymbol interference before equalisation.   It can be shown that, providing the initial unequalised intersymbol interference distortion $D_0 < 1$, then zero-forcing is optimum in minimising the post-equalisation intersymbol interference D.   If $D_0 \geq 1$, then a different optimisation criterion must be used.

In fact it is possible to completely eliminate the trailing response samples (those coming after I_0, the peak value) by connecting the equaliser coefficients recursively, that is , in a feed-back fashion as shown in Fig.1.14.

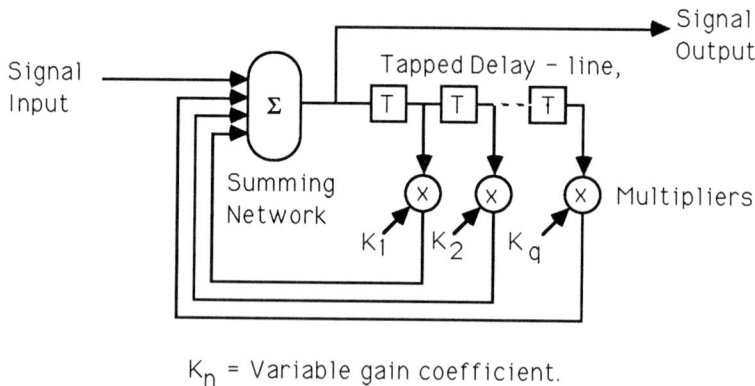

Fig.1.14 - Recursively connected equaliser configuration.

The pre-cursor response samples (those preceding I_0) still need to be equalised using a normal feed-forward connected transversal filter, otherwise the equaliser can become unstable due to feedback coefficients being greater than unity. Thus a network notionally as shown in Fig.1.15 would be appropriate. This really consists of two separate filter sections as demarcated by the dotted line in Fig.1.15.

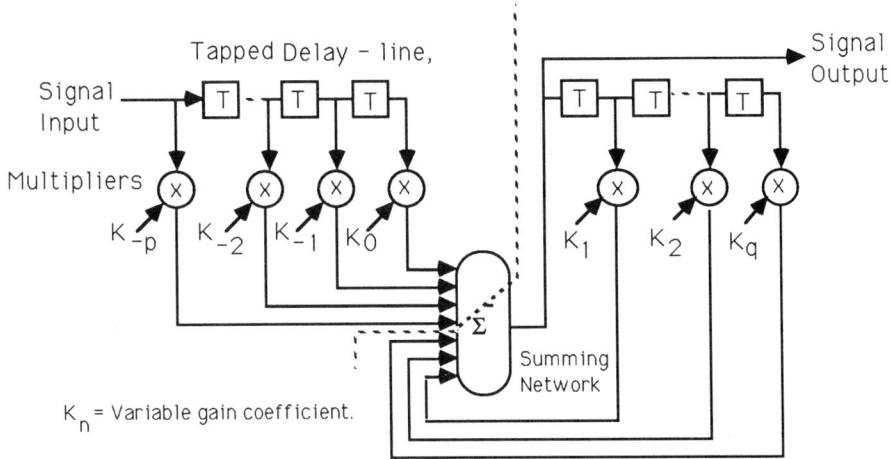

Fig.1.15 - Transversal equaliser with feedback taps.

Because the sections act separately on the signal, we can reverse the order of the two sections as shown in Fig.1.16(a). As the two delay-line sections now contain the same signal, this arrangement can then be simplified further into the 'canonical'.form shown in Fig.1.16(b), thus saving on the provision of delay elements in the implementation.

AUTOMATIC PRESET AND ADAPTIVE EQUALISERS

Frequently the transmission circuit to be used, and hence the channel characteristics are not known until the sender is ready to transmit data over the network. This is the case, for instance, for dial-up circuits through the public switched telephone network. This means that equalisation has to be carried out each time a circuit is acquired for data transmission purposes. An automatic setting-up procedure is therefore highly desirable.

Sometimes the circuit characteristics are time-varying at a rate which allows significant changes to take place in the period of time the circuit is occupied for data transmission purposes. Under these conditions it is necessary to make the equalisation process adaptive.

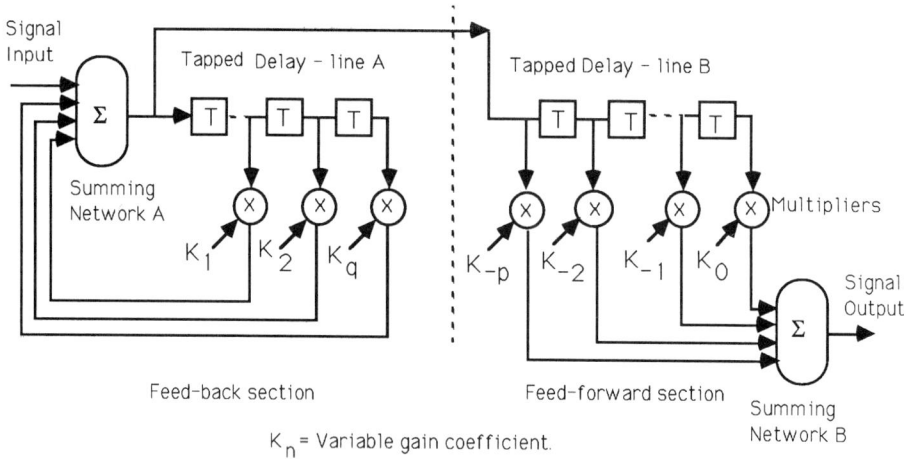

(a) Rearrangement of recursive equaliser

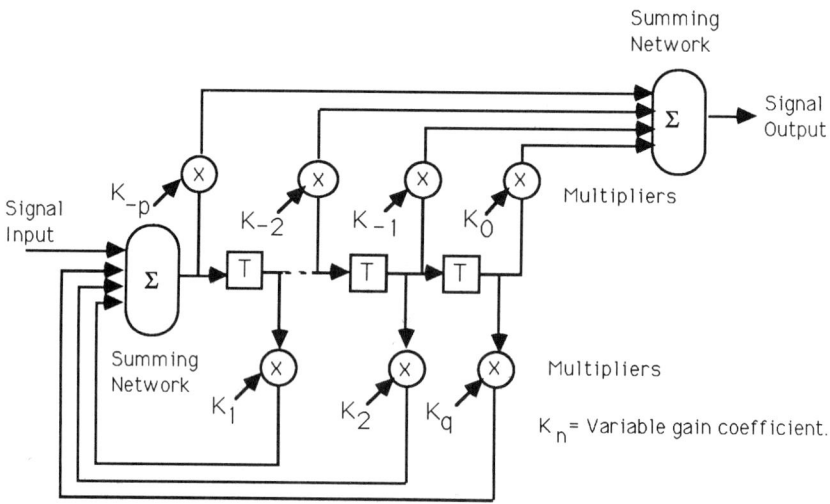

(b) Canonical recursive equaliser

Fig.1.16 - Recursive transversal equaliser configurations.

To automatically preset the equaliser, a test pattern is transmitted and the prior knowledge of the pattern at the receiver is used to compute the impulse response from the received signal. From the impulse response so obtained, it is then possible either to calculate the tap coefficients directly or to use an iterative technique to successively increment the coefficients until an optimum setting is obtained. The strategy is illustrated in Fig.1.17. This mode of operation gives fast initial setting-up but, if the channel characteristics are changing, it becomes necessary to retransmit the test pattern at intervals to allow for resetting of the coefficients. Fig.1.18 shows an alternative mode of operation generally referred to as adaptive equalisation. Instead of using a test pattern, the method is based on the assessment of the error between the actual received signal and the receiver

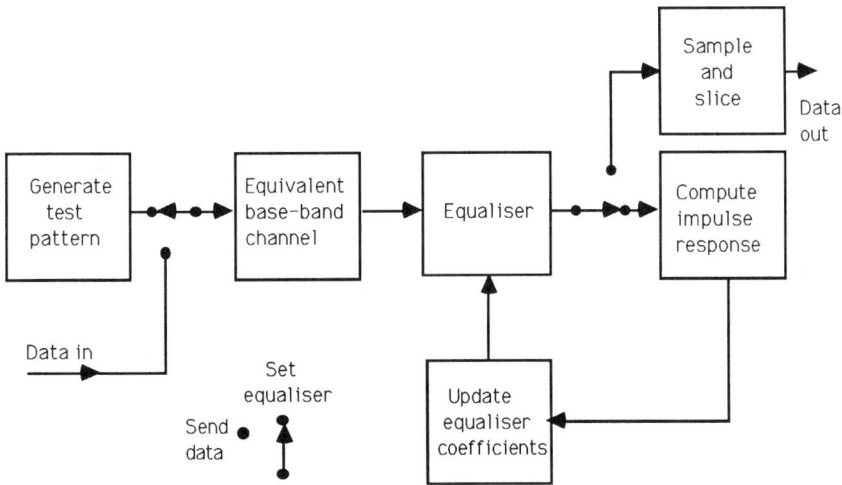

Fig.1.17 - Automatic pre-set equaliser strategy.

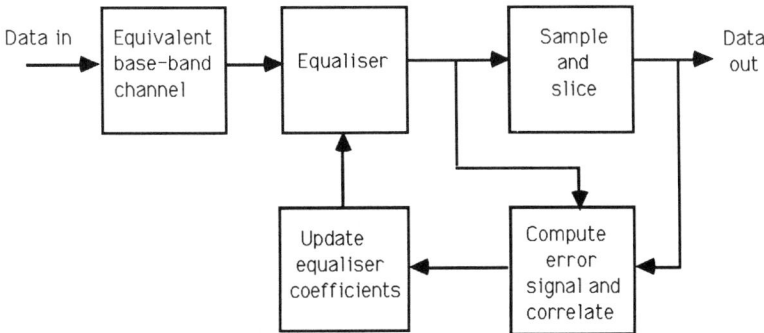

Fig.1.18 - Adaptive equaliser strategy.

estimate of the transmitted symbol. The error signal so obtained is correlated with the received data signal to obtain estimates of coefficient setting errors. The coefficients are then updated in accordance with these estimates so as to minimise the magnitude of the error signal. This strategy has the advantage that the setting-up procedure is a continually adapting feedback controlled process. However, if the unequalised signal is so badly distorted that a large proportion of erroneous decisions are made, the equaliser may not initially converge and equalisation will not be achieved. Under such conditions it is possible to start up in the preset mode, using an initial test pattern, and then to change to the adaptive mode when a reasonable degree of equalisation has been achieved.   The basic hardware for the adaptive equaliser is given in Fig.1.19.   Correlation consists of

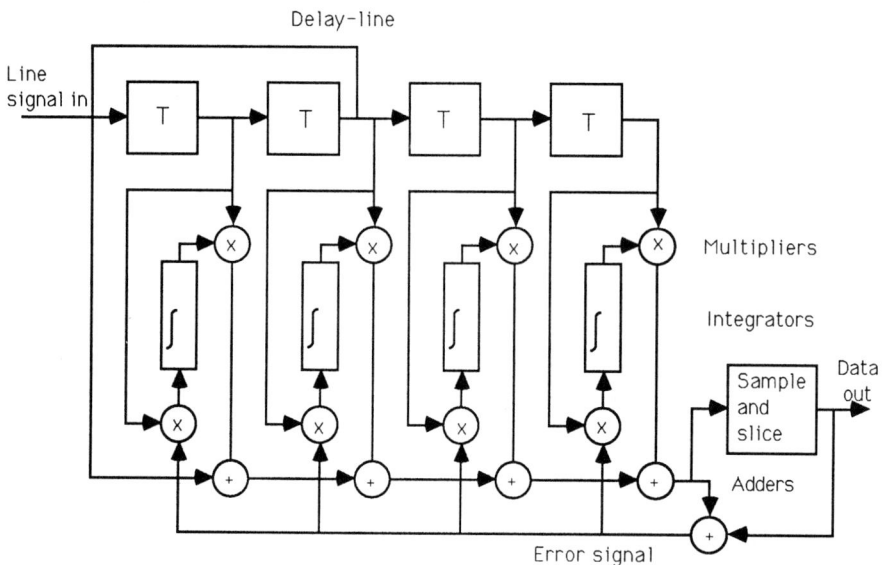

Fig.1.19 - Basic hardware for adaptive equaliser.

multiplying the error signal with the delayed signal at the appropriate coefficient multiplier input and integrating the product so formed.   In fact the integrator output forms the actual coefficient value, adapting until the mean value of the output of the output of the correlation multiplier becomes zero.   It can be shown that, provided the receiver estimate of the transmitted data is predominantly correct, then the equaliser coefficient values converge to minimise the mean-square error in the received signal, whether the error arises from intersymbol interference or from additive noise.

THE NEED FOR SCRAMBLING

The proper operation of an adaptive equaliser depends on the fact that the data source generates the binary data symbols completely randomly. In practice long strings of data can be generated that are anything but random. Rest conditions can involve the transmission of long strings of binary 0s or 1s or, perhaps, 'reversals' or 'dotting' patterns consisting of alternate 0s and 1s. Under such conditions it is impossible to obtain an estimate of the intersymbol interference by correlation because the signal samples do not possess the necessary statistical independence. It is desirable, therefore, to be able to produce random, or apparently random, strings of binary digits which may be used as test signals or for the purposes of data randomisation ('scrambling').

PSEUDO-RANDOM BINARY SEQUENCES

The usual method of generating an apparently random binary sequence is to use a sequential feed-back shift-register arrangement which will generate a maximal length pseudo-random binary sequence (p.r.b.s.), often referred to as an 'm' sequence.

Consider an n-stage shift-register with feed-back connections via exclusive-OR gates as shown in Fig.1.20, where C_k, k = 1 to n, takes the value 0 or 1.

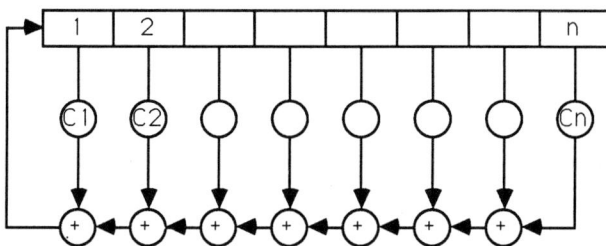

Fig.1.20 - N-stage feed-back shift-register.

By suitable choice of the values of the coefficients C_k, it is possible to make the shift-register cycle through all the possible n-tuples sequentially, except the all-zero n-tuple. If the register ever contains the all-zero n-tuple, then it will remain in this state indefinitely. The operation of the shift-register arrangement is dependent on its 'characteristic polynomial'. The characteristic polynomial is given by

$$\emptyset(x) = 1 + \sum_{k=1}^{n} C_k x^k$$

To obtain a maximal length sequence, the characteristic polynomial must be primitive. The powers of x in the characteristic polynomial either exist or do not exist, depending on whether the appropriate value of C is 1 or 0. Thus the powers of x that exist in the polynomial actually define the tap connections that are made in the shift-register. The characteristic polynomial is therefore often referred to as the tap polynomial. To minimise the hardware necessary to implement the m-sequence generator, it is obviously desirable to minimise the number of taps required to the shift-register. In fact, it is frequently possible to obtain a maximal-length sequence with only two tapping points, an intermediate point and the end of the shift-register. Unfortunately this cannot be done with a shift-register of length 8 and various other lengths greater than 8. These require a minimum of 4 tapping points, 3 intermediate and one at the end of the shift-register. Suitable

TABLE 1.1 - Characteristic polynomials for m-sequence generators.

n	polynomial	n	polynomial
3	$x^3 + x^2 + 1$	4	$x^4 + x^3 + 1$
5	$x^5 + x^3 + 1$	6	$x^6 + x^5 + 1$
7	$x^7 + x^6 + 1$	8	$x^8 + x^7 + x^2 + x + 1$
9	$x^9 + x^5 + 1$	10	$x^{10} + x^7 + 1$
11	$x^{11} + x^9 + 1$	12	$x^{12} + x^{11} + x^{10} + x^2 + 1$
13	$x^{13} + x^{12} + x^{11} + x + 1$	14	$x^{14} + x^{13} + x^{12} + x^2 + 1$
15	$x^{15} + x^{14} + 1$	16	$x^{16} + x^{14} + x^{13} + x^{11} + 1$
17	$x^{17} + x^{14} + 1$	18	$x^{18} + x^{11} + 1$
19	$x^{19} + x^{18} + x^{17} + x^{14} + 1$	20	$x^{20} + x^{17} + 1$

characteristic polynomials for shift-registers from length 3 to 20 are given in Table 1.1. These are not the only primitive polynomials for each length of shift-register but they do make use of the minimum possible number of tapping points. An example of a 9-stage shift-register p.r.b.s. generator is given in Fig.1.21. Note that for single intermediate tapping-point sequence generators, it turns out that the use of the intermediate feed-back point (n - m) instead of m will generate a similar sequence of length $2^n - 1$, but in the reverse order.

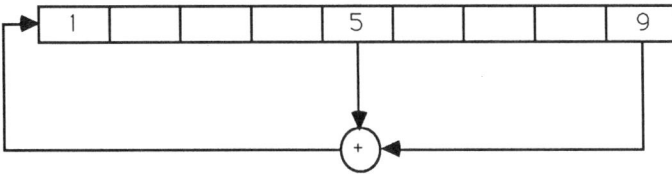

Fig.1.21 - 9-stage p.r.b.s. generator.

The output from a pseudo-random sequence generator can be used as a 'test' signal to set up an automatic equaliser before transmission of actual data. The length of the sequence should be chosen so that it is significantly greater than the impulse response of the channel and the equaliser together, to maintain statistical independence over all coefficients. Typically 7 or 9-bit shift-register generators are adequate, giving sequences of span 127 and 511 respectively. 8-bit shift-registers are not usually chosen as they require additional feed-back logic, there being no primitive polynomial of order 8 with only one intermediate term.

SELF-SYNCHRONISING SCRAMBLERS/DESCRAMBLERS

For adaptive equalisers it is necessary to use the pseudo-random sequence concept to randomise (scramble) the transmitted data sequence. It is also necessary to be able to descramble the sequence on receipt! One way of doing this would be to simply add, modulo-2, the data and the sequence generated by an independent shift-register generator. However, to descramble, it will be necessary to have an identical shift-register generator at the receiver, operating in the same phase, in order to effect the descrambling. The problem is how to obtain and then to maintain the same sequence phase at both the transmitter and the receiver.   To avoid this problem, the self-synchronising scambler-descrambler combination is used.   The

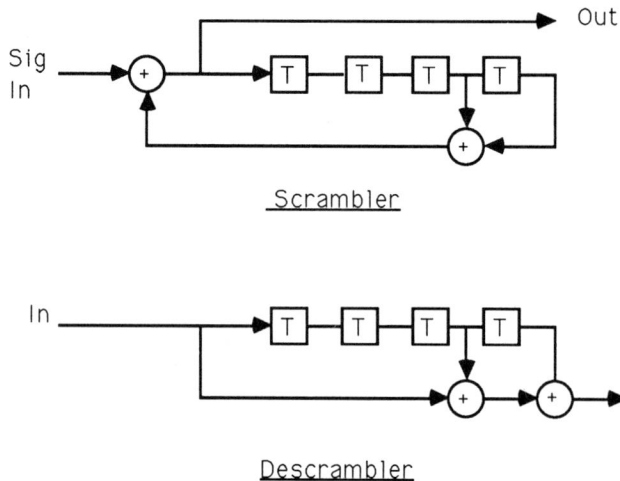

Fig.1.22 - Self-synchronising scrambler-descrambler.

scrambler and the descrambler each consist of a shift-register similar to that used for the p.r.b.s. generator, but the signals to be operated on are introduced directly into the feed-back path as shown in Fig.1.22. The mathematics relating to the scrambler operation are beyond the scope of this book, but the interested reader is referred to Savage's original paper (listed in the bibliography) for a full treatment. However, with patience, it is a fairly simple matter to verify the operation, at least for a fairly short scrambler, using the pragmatic approach. Clearly, with an all-zero input, the scrambler in effect becomes a conventional p.r.b.s. generator. Savage has shown that, for a periodic signal input, the line sequence period will be the lowest common multiple (LCM) of the corresponding p.r.b.s. and the input signal periods.

    There is a small, but finite, chance of 'lock-up' if the all-zero sequence enters the register and is then maintained by an all-zero input. The larger n, the smaller this probability becomes and, for typical scrambler shift-register lengths of 22, it can safely be neglected.   It will be seen that the sequence input into both the scrambler and descrambler shifft-registers are identical (assuming no errors in transmission) and thus the two will be synchronised once n bits have been transmitted through the channel.   This usually occurs during set-up, so no data is lost in practice during this synchronisation interval.

If an errror occurs in transmission, it will affect the descrambled data as it passes through each tapping point of the shift-register.   For this reason it is important to minimise, as far as possible, the number of taps used.   Using the polynomials with minimum taps, each error in transmission will give rise to up to three errors in the descrambler output.   This error propagation is one of the penalties we have to pay for the convenience of using the self-synchronising data scrambler-descrambler.   Almost all high-speed data transmission equipment incorporates scrambling since it not only ensures proper operation of automatic adaptive equalisers, but it also ensures adequate polarity transitions in the data sequence from which timing and synchronisation information can be obtained when long strings of '0' or '1' are being sent.

2

Modems and the Datel services.

MODULATION OF DATA SIGNALS

The ubiquitous nature of the telephone network makes it an attractive medium for the transmission of data signals. However, basic data signals generally do not exist in a form that is suitable for direct transmission over telephone connections. For instance, the normal telephone connection is not a low-pass circuit since the speech circuits are a.c coupled and the d.c. path, where it exists, is used exclusively for signalling purposes. Since a typical data signal has significant frequency components near to d.c., it is therefore impossible to carry such signals directly over the telephone network. To combat this problem, modulation - demodulation equipment is used. Such equipment is usually referred to as a 'modem'. The modem converts data signals to frequencies in the voice-band which are suitable for transmission over the telephone network and on reception recovers the transmitted data sequence from the received signal. In the UK, data services provided by British Telecom using modems over the public telephone network are designated the DATEL services.

FREQUENCY-SHIFT KEYING

For low-speed data applications frequency-shift-keying (FSK) is a reliable and easily implemented modulation scheme in which the binary data 0s and 1s are represented by bursts of 'carrier' signal at two frequencies f_1 and f_2, respectively.

The principle of FSK modulation is illustrated in Fig.2.1. Unfortunately FSK does not make the best use of the available channel bandwidth and is thus not suitable for high-speed data applications. The first modems to be introduced into service were FSK modems. FSK was chosen because it gave a good performance, providing stable operation over a wide variety of channels, permitted asynchronous

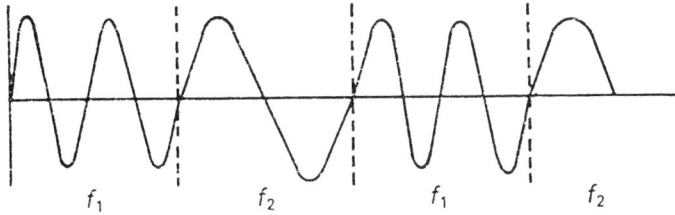

Fig.2.1 - Example of FSK modulation.

operation and was reasonably simple to implement. Additionally, the FSK modem performance is not affected in any way by the data sequence because the line signal is always present with constant amplitude whatever the pattern of 1s and 0s.

Two standard FSK modems are in general use. The first was designed to enable keyboards and similar machines to communicate over the public switched telephone network (PSTN) and private speech circuits at signalling rates of up to 200 bits/s in a full duplex mode. CCITT recommendation V21 was established to cover this requirement internationally and made provision for a possible extension of the rate up to 300 bits/s in each direction. The frequency allocation chosen is given in Table 2.1. Channel 1 is used for the transmission of the caller's data while channel 2 is used for the transmission in the other direction. Asynchronous or synchronous working between data equipments is possible when using these modems. The service offered by BT using this modem is referred to as DATEL 200.

Table 2.1 - Characteristic frequencies for V21 modems operating at 200 bits/s over PSTN circuits.

Channel	Nominal mean frequency (Hz)	Binary symbol 1 frequency (Hz)	Binary symbol 0 frequency (Hz)
1	1080	980	1180
2	1750	1650	1850

The second standard was introduced to provide a higher-speed link, the main use of which has been to enable visual display units to be serviced by a host computer with greater rapidity than was possible by the previously described modem. A low-speed return channel, which could allow control signals or telegraph-type keyboard signals to be transmitted, was provided as an option if required. The modem again operated on either the public switched telephone network or private speech circuits, this time at data signalling rates of up to 1200 bits/s. However, with a small proportion of the poorer quality switched network connections, difficulty was experienced in obtaining 1200 bits/s and so a fall-back facility was provided to enable operation at 600 bits/s to be assured over the PSTN. The return channel operates at modulation rates of up to 75 bits/s. The frequency allocation for this modem is given in Table 2.2. The international standard is established in CCITT recommendation V23 and the service offered by BT using this modem is referred to as DATEL 600.

For data signalling rates in excess of 1200 bits/s, techniques which make more efficient use of the available bandwidth have to be employed. Examples of modulation schemes in current use which require less line bandwidth than FSK for a given modulation rate are Phase-Shift Keying (PSK) and Quadrature-Amplitude Modulation (QAM).

Table 2.2 - Characteristic frequencies for V23 modems operating at 600/1200 bits/s.

Mode	Nominal mean frequency (Hz)	Binary symbol 1 frequency (Hz)	Binary symbol 0 frequency (Hz)
1 (up to 600 bits/s)	1500	1300	1700
2 (up to 1200 bits/s	1700	1300	2100
Optional return channel (75 bits/s)	420	390	450

PHASE-SHIFT KEYING

Phase-shift keying involves taking n bits at a time from the data sequence and encoding them into 2^n phase-shifts of a single-frequency carrier. The principle of PSK modulation is illustrated in Fig.2.2. The phasor diagram for a 4-phase PSK signal is given in Fig. 2.3. Note that 2 bits are encoded into each phase, since $2^2 = 4$.

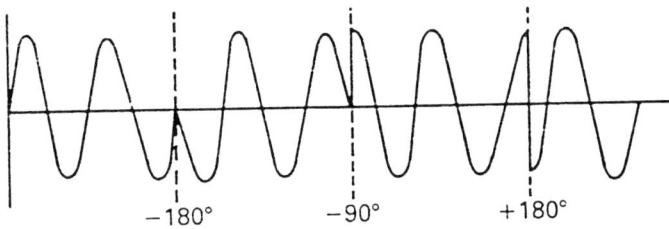

Fig 2.2 - Example of PSK modulation.

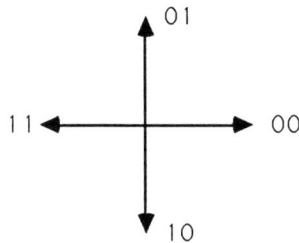

Fig.2.3 - Phasor diagram for 4-phase PSK.

Similarly, an 8-phase signal will encode 3 bits of data per change of carrier phase. Signal constellation diagrams for 4-phase and 8-phase PSK signals are given in Fig. 2.4

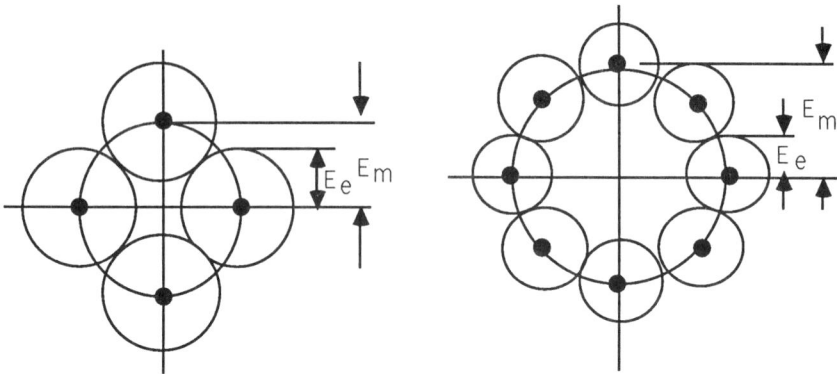

Fig.2.4 - Signal constellation diagram, 4-phase and 8-phase PSK.

In practice PSK is rarely used in its basic form since a reference carrier is needed at the receiver with which to compare the received signal. Providing a suitable reference is technically very difficult to achieve. Instead of encoding into a phase-shift that has an absolute relationship to some arbitary reference, one can encode the various data combinations (symbols) into phase changes, relative to that transmitted in the previous symbol epoch. Thus no absolute phase reference is required at the receiver. The receiver simply observes the phase changes at each symbol interval and decodes accordingly. This technique is known as differential phase-shift keying (DPSK). There is, of course, a slight penalty to be paid for this simplification. If, due to noise or some other signal impairment, an erroneous decision regarding a particular symbol is taken, then the next symbol will also be read in error, even though its phase is detected correctly, because it will be compared to an erroneous reference in the decoding process. Thus the expected error-rate for a DPSK system is twice that theoretically obtainable using PSK. However, the comparative simplicity of implementation far outwieghs the cost in terms of error performance.

The first requirement for a data rate greater than 1200 bits/s was met by a modem designed to operate at 2400 bits/s. Originally this modem, to CCITT recommendation V26, was intended for operation over four-wire private speech-band circuits. However, a variant (V26 bis) was subsequently introduced for use over the public switched telephone network. This variant was provided with a fall-back facility to 1200 bits/s where the line characteristics were unsuitable for 2400 bits/s operation. The modem operated at a modulation rate of 1200 bauds, the data being taken in pairs of bits and being conveyed as one of four possible phase-shifts of a 1800 Hz carrier. The four-phase signal is differentially encoded. The significance of the phase changes is given in Table 2.3. The two alternatives are available for the leased-line modem (V26) but the switched network modem (V26 bis) is only available using alternative B. The adavantage of alternative B is that there is always a phase-change between adjacent modulation epochs.

Table 2.3 - Line-signal phase changes for V26 differential four-phase modem.

Pair of data signal elements (dibit)	Phase change (degrees)	
	Alternative A	Alternative B
00	0	+ 45
01	+ 90	+135
11	+180	+225
10	+270	+315

The nature of the four-phase differential modulation techniques used in this modem, in which pairs of data signal-elements are identified by phase changes of carrier signal, requires that the tranmission be synchronous, i.e. that both the modulator and demodulator, together with the data terminal equipment, must be controlled by timimg signals in such a way that the individual data-signal elements can be correctly identified in the demodulation process. The service is offered by British Telecom under the title Datel 2400.

Following the successful operation of 2400 bits/s modems the next requirement is for 4800 bits/s operation. This is achieved by the use of differential eight-phase modulation on a 1800 Hz carrier at a modulation rate of 1600 bauds. Equalisation is necessary in order to obtain satisfactory operation at this data rate. Three alternatives have been recommended by CCITT as follows:

V27   4800 bits/s modem with manually set equaliser for use on high quality leased voice-band circuits.

V27 bis   4800 bits/s modem with automatic adaptive equaliser and fall-back facility to 2400 bits/s operation in accordance with recommendation V26A for use on general quality leased voice-band circuits.

V27 ter   4800 bits/s modem with automatic adaptive equaliser and fall-back facility to 2400 bits/s operation in accordance with recommendation V26A for operation over the public switched telephone network.

The significance of the phase changes for each of these options is given in Table 2.4.

Table 2.4 - Line signal phase changes for differential eight-phase modems.

Tribit value	Phase change (degrees)
001	+0
000	+45
010	+90
011	+135
111	+180
110	+225
100	+270
101	+315

EQUIVALENT BASE-BAND CHANNEL AND EQUALISATION

If the modulation and demodulation techniques used in the modem equipment are linear operations, then the band-pass transmission channel in combination with the modulator and demodulator behaves externally just like a low-pass channel. The equivalence is shown in Fig.2.5. This enables the techniques regarding channel shaping and equalisation described in the previous chapter to be applied to the equivalent base-band channel consisting of the band-pass channel and modem equipment.

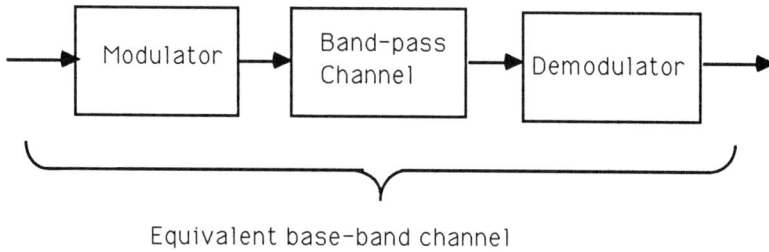

Fig.2.5 - Equivalent base-band channel.

QUADRATURE AMPLITUDE MODULATION

The margin of error in decoding a PSK or DPSK signal is indicated in Fig.2.4 by the radius of the circles E_e around each point in the signal constellation. Any noise perturbation of the signal greater in amplitude than E_e is likely to cause the signal to be erroneously decoded. Obviously, as the number of phases is increased, so the margin of error rapidly decreases. There is thus a limit to the number of phases that can usefully be employed and, in practice, this turns out to be about 8. However, by choice of a different signal constellation, it is possible to increase the margin of error for a greater number of signal points in the constellation. Compare the signal constellation diagram for 8-phase PSK given in Fig.2.4 with that for 16-point quadrature amplitude modulation (QAM) given in Fig.2.6. Clearly the latter has a comparable error performance despite being able to convey data at a significantly higher rate. QAM consists of two independent amplitude-modulated signals having the same carrier frequency but with carriers 90° out of phase with each other, that is, in quadrature ($\sin 2\pi f_c t$ and $\cos 2\pi f_c t$). Because carriers in quadrature are orthogonal, they can be demodulated independently using appropriate quadrature demodulating carriers as shown in Fig.2.7.

The result is equivalent to a base-band channel that is capable of handling simultaneously a pair of waveforms or, alternatively, as two separate base-band channels using a single transmission path. An error in demodulating carrier phase will cause some cross-modulation between the two signals, creating cross-channel intersymbol interference. This can be eliminated by the use of equalisation

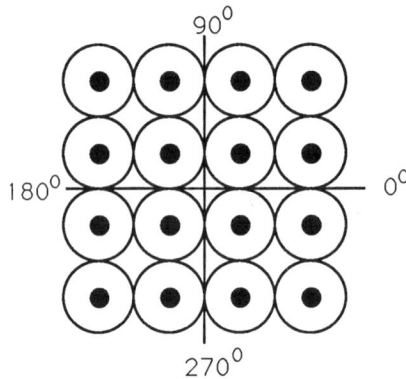

Fig.2.6 - Signal constellation for 16-state QAM.

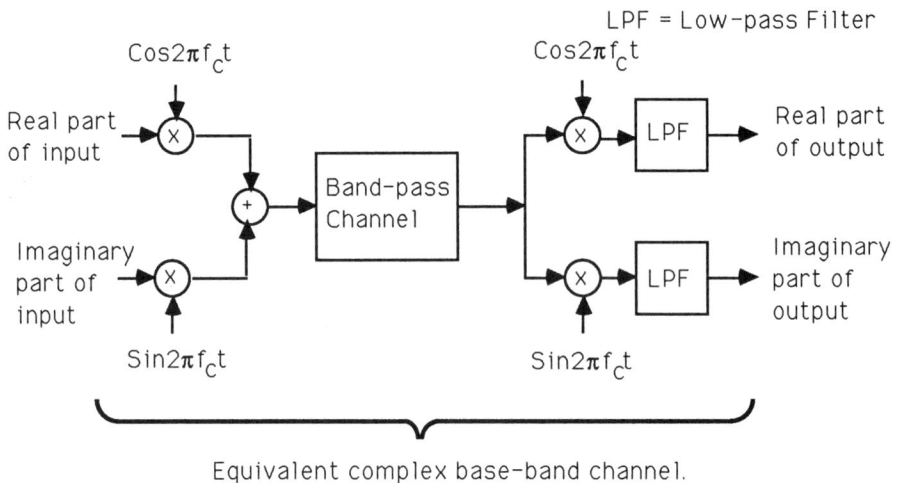

Fig 2.7 - Quadrature amplitude modulation system.

techniques similar to those described in chapter 1 to deal with the intersymbol interference caused by pulse dispersion. In fact the two functions are normally combined in a single device referred to as a complex channel equaliser. The reason for this title will become clearer when we have described the function of the device in more detail. A schematic diagram of the QAM complex equaliser is given in Fig.2.8.

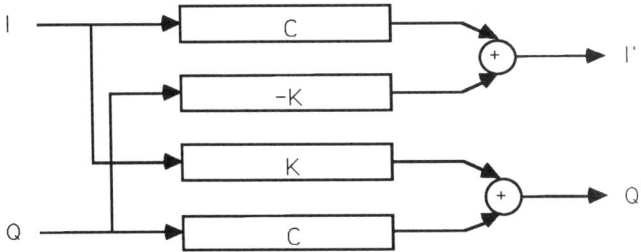

$$(I + jQ).(C + jK) = (CI - KQ) + j(CQ + KI)$$
$$= I' \qquad + jQ'$$

Fig.2.8 - QAM equaliser.

The two equivalent base-band channel sampled outputs are given by the vectors I and Q. Since both use the same physical channel with the same carrier frequency, we would expect the channel impulse responses to be identical. The coefficient arrays C for the two transversal filters equalising the channel intersymbol interference will therefore be identical. To cancel the cross-channel intersymbol interference, appropriately weighted delayed versions of the quadrature channel signal are added to the reference phase channel signal and vice versa, the weighting coefficient arrays taking the values -K and K respectively. The reason for the opposite polarities of the K values for the two channels is that the effect of carrier phase-error is complementary in the two channels rather than identical. This opposite polarity effect makes it convenient to represent the channel output signals I and Q and the coefficient arrays C and K as complex mathematical quantities as shown in Fig.2.8. Hence the title 'complex' equaliser. The equaliser is thus able to cope with phase errors. In fact, applying the adaptive techniques described in chapter 1 to the complex equaliser, it is possible for the complex equaliser to track a continuously changing phase error caused by a small error in the demodulating carrier frequency. The complex equaliser is therefore a very powerful tool for use in conjunction with QAM modems.

A number of QAM modems for use over telephone lines have been implemented. Successful transmission has been achieved with a 64 point (8 x 8) constellation using adaptive equalisation to obtain a data rate of 19.2 kbits/s. A 9.6 kbits/s modem to CCITT recommendation V29 uses a form of QAM, but does not use all points in the constellation.   The reason for the choice is that fall-back to standard CCITT phase-modulation (PSK) schemes is possible if the line quality is not good enough to achieve 9.6 kbits/s using QAM.   However, the techniques used are identical to the QAM scheme descibed above.   The constellation used is given in Fig.2.9.

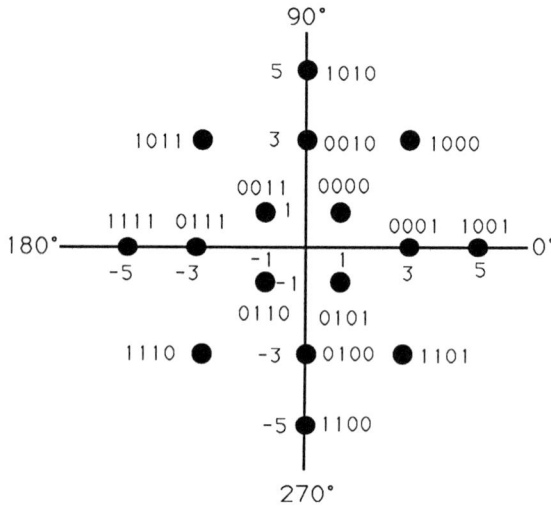

Fig.2.9 - Signal space constellation for 9600 bits/s V29 modem.

Baseband modems and line codes

INTRODUCTION

Modulation is not the only method of signal processing that can be used to match the spectrum of the transmitted signal to that of the available channel bandwidth. By using various coding techniques, known as line codes, it is often possible to produce a suitable line spectrum without having to resort to the more complex procedure of modulation. Neither the simple bipolar binary code, where a 1 is represented by a positive pulse and 0 is represented by a negative pulse, nor the simple unipolar binary code, where 1 is represented by a positive pulse and 0 is represented by no signal, is ideal for line transmission purposes. Both suffer from the existence of strong frequency components at low frequencies and a lack of signal transitions when long strings of identical symbols are transmitted sequentially. These transitions are necessary to derive timing signals for the reciver decoder to enable the decoder to determine the number of consecutive bits in the sequence. To overcome these problems, line codes have been developed which have properties which make them particularly useful for line transmission.

The desirable features of a line code are as follows:

(a) *Tranparency.* The code must not impose any restriction on the content of the transmitted message, i.e. it must be bit-sequence-independent.

(b) *Unique decodability.* Each output symbol must be unambiguously decoded to give the original sequence of input bits.

(c) *Efficiency.* Each symbol of the code should contribute to the transmission of the incoming information.

(d) *Favourable energy spectrum.* The presence of transformer and coupling capacitors in the system requires the line code to have a d.c. component averaging zero and very small low-frequency components. Since cross-channel interference caused by coupling between adjacent circuits increases with frequency, interference power can be reduced by minimising the high frequency content of the transmitted signals.

(e) *Timing information content.*   It is desirable that the spectrum of the transmitted signal has a high energy content close to the data clock frequency.   This will be obtained if the line signal has frequent transitions at the clock interval.

(f) *Low digital sum variation (DSV).*   If we define a running digital sum (RDS) as

$$RDS(k) = \sum_{n=1}^{k} C_n + RDS(0),$$

where C_n = 1, 0 or -1 for a ternary signal (or ± 1 for binary), and RDS(0) is an appropriately chosen constant, the DSV is then given by

$$DSV = RDS(Max) - RDS(Min).$$

The higher the DSV, the greater the concentration of signal energy around the low frequency end of the spectrum and the fewer transitions in the transmitted line signal.   Those codes with the lowest DSV are therefore to be preferred.   The DSV is often referred to as the code disparity.

BINARY LINE CODES

Line codes for binary data transmission generally divide into two types. The first type are still binary in nature, but the code structure is modified to improve the code properties. Two such codes are the Walsh function codes Wal 1 and Wal 2. These are illustrated in Fig.3.1(a).   In both cases the line signal is free from d.c. component and contains a large number of transitions from which timing information can be recovered, whatever the transmitted data pattern. The line code spectra for random binary data using these two codes are shown in Fig.3.1(b), where they are compared with the spectrum for the simple bipolar binary code.   In both cases the spectrum has no d.c. component and small low-frequency

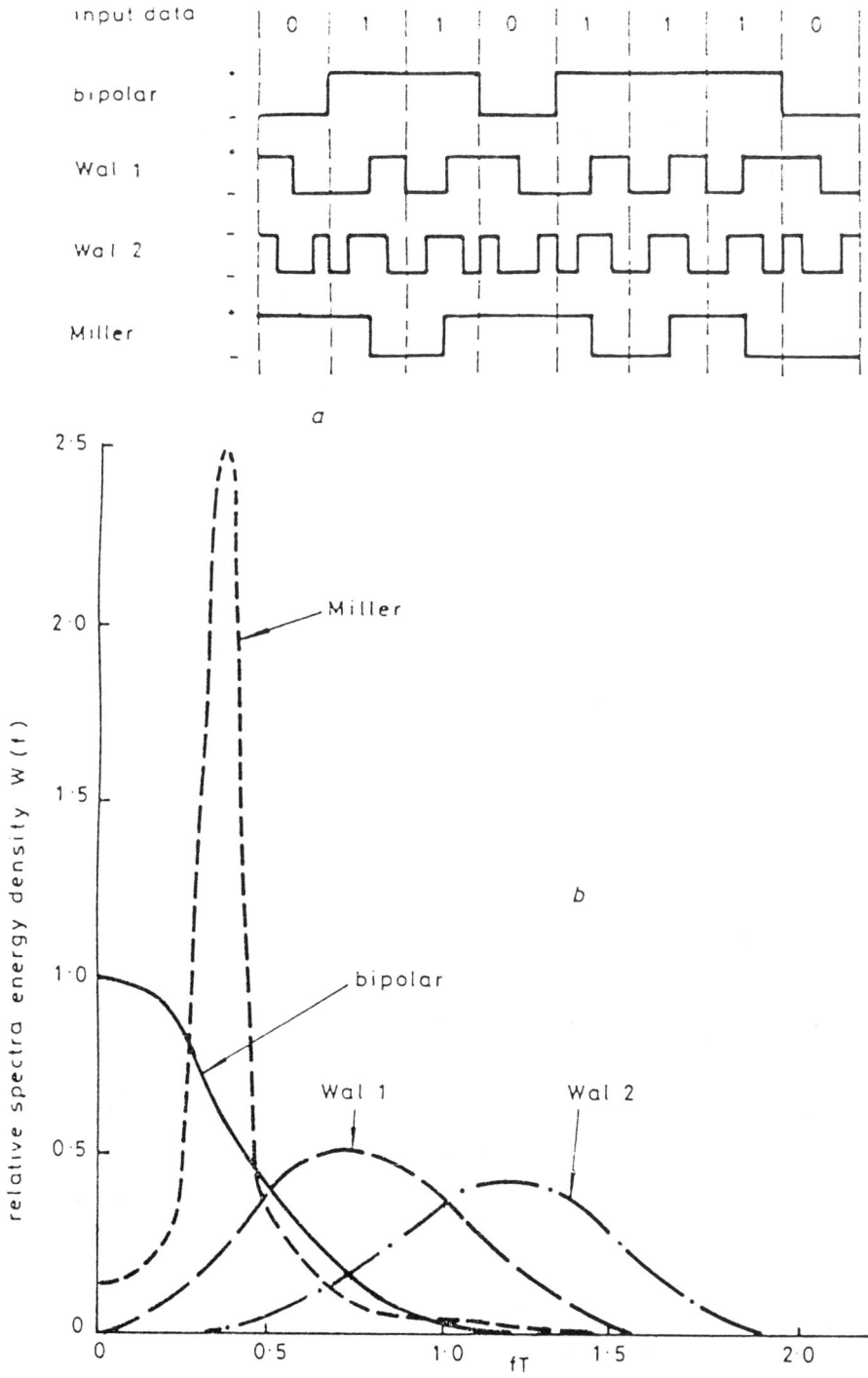

Fig.3.1 - Binary codes based on Wal 1 and Wal 2. (a) Transmitted waveform. (b) Line spectra.

components.   The band-width occupancy of the Wal 2 coded signal is slightly
greater than for Wal 1, extending to approximately twice the transmission rate. The
Wal 2 spectrum has no significant content below 0.2 of the transmission rate, a fact
that can be made use of in data-over-voice applications. Another useful code is the
Miller code, or delay modulation, as it is sometimes called. This code is a variation
of the Wal 1 and is derived by deleting every second transition in a Wal 1 signal, as
illustrated in Fig.3.1(a).   The spectrum shape of the line signal is given in
Fig.3.1(b), where it is compared with the Wal 1 and Wal 2 spectra. Although it has
a small d.c. component, it has the advantage of a more limited bandwidth
requirement than the comparable Wal codes.   The Wal 1 code is sometimes
referred to as Manchester encoding.

TERNARY LINE CODES

The second type of line codes are ternary codes which operate on three signal levels,
the middle level of which is usually zero volts. These codes are sometimes referred
to as pseudo-ternary since, although the code has three levels and therefore an
information bearing capability greater than binary coding, each ternary symbol is
used to convey only one bit of information. The best known of the pseudo-ternary
codes is alternate mark inversion (AMI).   The encoded sequence is obtained by
representing the marks (1s) in the binary sequence alternately by positive and
negative impulses, whilst the spaces (0s) are represented by no signal. The code
structure and its line signal power spectrum are illustrated in Fig.3.2.   The AMI
code has some very attractive properties. The line signal power density spectrum
has no d.c. component and very small low-frequency spectrum content. The code
disparity is equal to 1. The coding and decoding circuitry requirements are quite
simple and some degree of error monitoring can be achieved by simply observing
violations of the AMI rule. It has the disadvantage that it has poor timing content
associated with long runs of binary zeros.

LINEAR PSEUDO-TERNARY CODES

There are some useful codes that fall within the subclass of linear pseudo-ternary

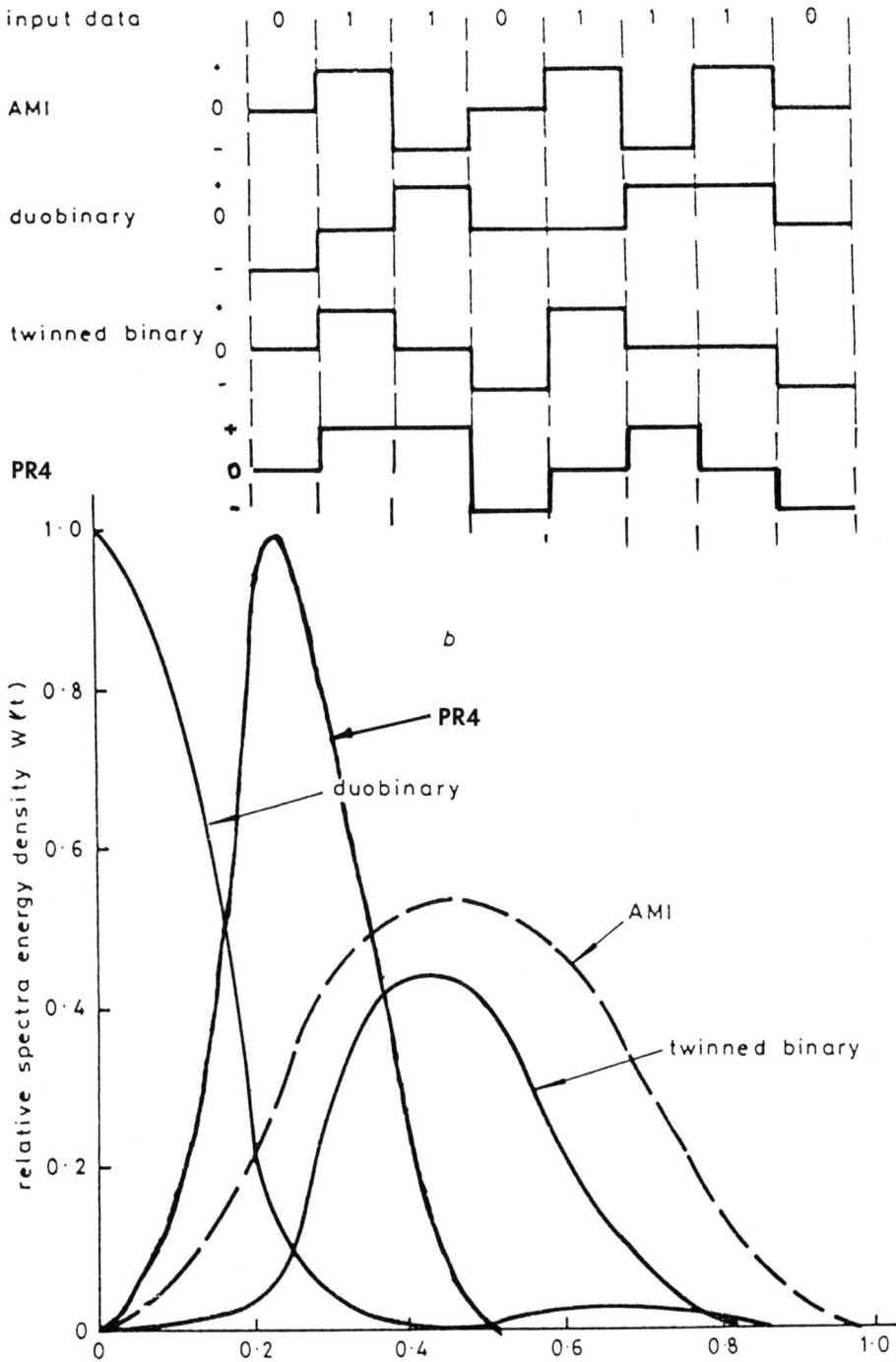

Fig.3.2 - AMI and linear pseudo-ternary codes. (a) Transmitted waveforms. (b) Line spectra.

codes. These codes are designated linear because the pseudo-ternary code is linearly derived directly from the binary message. A linear pseudo-ternary code is actually a particular case of a binary code in which the signal element $S_0'(t)$ has been replaced by

$$S_t'(t) = S_1(t) \times S_0(t) ,$$

where $S_1(t)$ is the sequence of impulses

$$S_t(t) = \sum_{k=0}^{K} \alpha_k (t - kT) \tag{3.1}$$

Linear pseudo-ternary encoding can thus be considered as equivalent to a filtering operation, the frequency response of the equivalent filter being given by the Fourier transform of $S_1(t)$

$$S_1(\omega) = \sum_{k=0}^{K} \alpha_k e^{-jkT}$$

In order for the coded signal to have only three possible values for any input binary sequence it is necessary that there be only two $\alpha_k \neq 0$ and that they are either equal or opposite. We thus have two basic pseudo-ternary codes, the twinned binary, in which $\alpha_0 = -1/2$ and $\alpha_1 = +1/2$ (or the other way round), and the duobinary code, in which $\alpha_0 = \alpha_1 = +1/2$. The AMI and linear pseudo-ternary codes are illustrated in Fig.3.2, together with the power spectra for random data using these codes. The duobinary code has all its energy concentrated at low frequencies and has a very strong d.c. component. However, since the signal spectrum bandwidth is equal to only half the data rate, the code is attractive for use in limited bandwidth applications. The twinned binary code bandwidth is equal to the transmission rate and most of the signal energy is concentrated around half the bit-rate. The spectrum is thus very similar to that of AMI code. The code has an error-detecting capability since it obeys the AMI rule. It is, however, sensitive to errror in the decoding operation due to error propagation in the decoding circuit.

Both the Duobinary and the twinned binary codes are easily generated and decoded using the circuit arrangement shown in Fig.3.3. Note that the coefficient

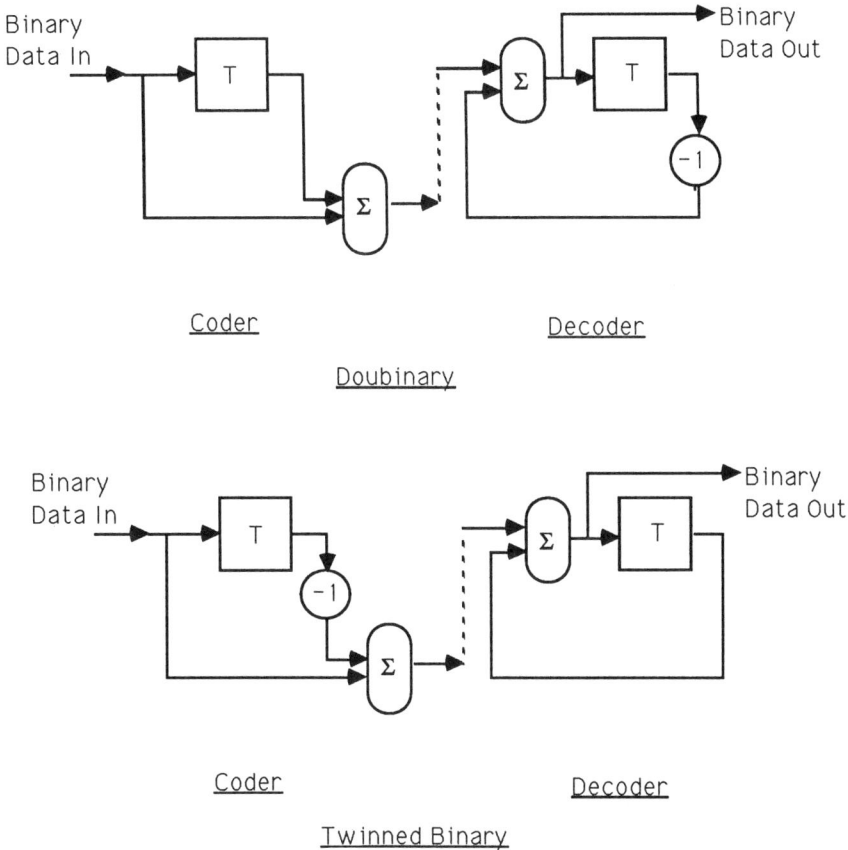

Fig.3.3 - Linear pseudo-ternary coders and decoders.

values shown in the practical circuits have the values +1 or -1 rather than +1/2 or -1/2. This simply scales the amplitude of the line signal by a factor of 2 and does not in any way alter the shape of the line signal or of its spectrum.

The linear pseudo-ternary codes are, in fact, special cases of the more general linear codes known as partial response codes. The partial response codes have been categorised by Kretzmer into a number of classes. In general, the partial response codes give more than 3 amplitude levels in the line signal. Kretzmer's class 1 partial response, however, is in fact the duobinary coding described above. One other partial response code is of interest to us since it also yields 3 levels in the line signal. This code is the partial response class 4 (PR4) code. In the PR4 code, the values of α_k in equation (3.1) are $\alpha_0 = +1/2$ and $\alpha_2 = -1/2$, with all the other α_k = 0. This has a line code spectrum that has zero d.c. component similar to the twinned binary code but the spectrum width is half that of twinned binary. It thus shares the advantages of both twinned binary and duobinary coding. It does, however, extend the effect of each binary symbol over the span of three line symbols, giving some error extension effects on the received and decoded signal. The twinned binary circuit given in Fig.3.4 can easily be amended for PR4 by simply increasing the delay in both the coder and decoder to 2T instead of T.

The other partial response codes have found little application as line codes because the increased number of levels that have to be distinguished in the line signal make them more vulnerable to error due to noise. Also the advantages to be gained in reduced bandwidth decreases very rapidly with increasing number of levels in the line code.

ALPHABETIC TERNARY CODES

There are also two classes of non-linear ternary codes which have application in the field of data transmission, namely alphabetic and non-alphabetic codes. In the alphabetic codes, n binary digits are taken together giving a signal element which can be regarded as a selection from an alphabet of 2^n possible characters. The character is then encoded into m ternary digits where $3^m > 2^n$. Such codes are normally described as 'nBmT codes'. The simplest of these codes is given by n = m = 2 and is generally known as 'pair selected ternary' (PST). The message signal is grouped in 2-bit words which are then coded in ternary as given in Table 3.1.

It can be seen there is no change in the rate of transmission. As each word is selected, the appropriate Word Digital Sum is added to a running sum total. The mode of the next ternary transmission is determined by the polarity of this running total. If the sum is negative, mode A is selected and if positive, mode B is selected. Where the total is equal to zero, the mode remains unchanged. Under normal conditions the running total will thus never vary more than 1 from the zero value and will alternate between positive and negative polarity when taking a value other than zero. Thus the PST code has a disparity of 2. The d.c. component in the transmitted signal is effectively reduced by the alternating mode, which is equivalent to the alternating polarity of AMI coding. Timing content is assured by the translation of pairs of zeros into pulses. The mode alternation also provides some error monitoring capability. The average power spectrum is given in Fig.3.4. The drawbacks of the code are that it has high low-frequency components and the transmission power is about 1.5 times that of AMI for similar performance.

Table 3.1 - PST code translation

Binary word	Ternary word		
	Mode A	Mode B	Word digital sum
00	- +	- +	0
01	0 +	0 -	±1
10	+ 0	+ 0	±1
11	+ -	+ -	0

Word synchronisation is also required by the coder in order to divide the received signal into the appropriate pairs for decoding purposes.

The ternary codes discussed so far are pseudo-ternary inasmuch as each ternary symbol only has a binary significance. A true ternary code is capable of conveying $\log_2 3$ bits of information per symbol rather than the binary rate of 1 bit per symbol.

The psuedo-ternary codes are thus only 63 per cent efficient in transmission capability, although the redundancy may give some error-detecting capability to the code. For example, in AMI, violations of the AMI rule would indicate that some error in transmission had occurred.

The efficency of transmission can be improved by the use of alphabetic codes where m < n. A widely used code of this class is that known as '4B3T'. The original binary data stream is divided into words of four bits, each word being encoded into three ternary digits as shown in Table 3.2.

Table 3.2 - 4B3T code translation

Binary word	Ternary code		Word digital sum
	Mode A	Mode B	
0000	+ 0 -	+ 0 -	0
0001	- + 0	- + 0	0
0010	0 - +	0 - +	0
0011	+ - 0	+ - 0	0
0100	+ + -	- - +	±2
0101	0 + +	0 - -	±2
0110	+ 0 +	- 0 -	±2
0111	+ + +	- - -	±3
1000	+ + -	- - +	±1
1001	- + +	+ - -	±1
1010	+ - +	- + -	±1
1011	+ 0 0	- 0 0	±1
1100	0 + 0	0 - 0	±1
1101	0 0 +	0 0 -	±1
1110	0 + -	0 + -	0
1111	- 0 +	- 0 +	0

The mode alternation is governed by the same rules as used for the PST code. The code gives a possibility of runs of similar digits up to a maximum of 6. Computing the running sum on a digit by digit basis, the code disparity is 8. However, if the running sum is only observed at the end of each of the ternary code groups, then the maximum sum variation is restricted to 6. The average power spectrum of the 4B3T code with random data is given in Fig.3.4. The power is fairly evenly distributed throughout the spectral band but there is a significantly large component at the low-frequency end of the spectrum. Some attempts to overcome this large low-frequency component have been made by the intoduction of modified

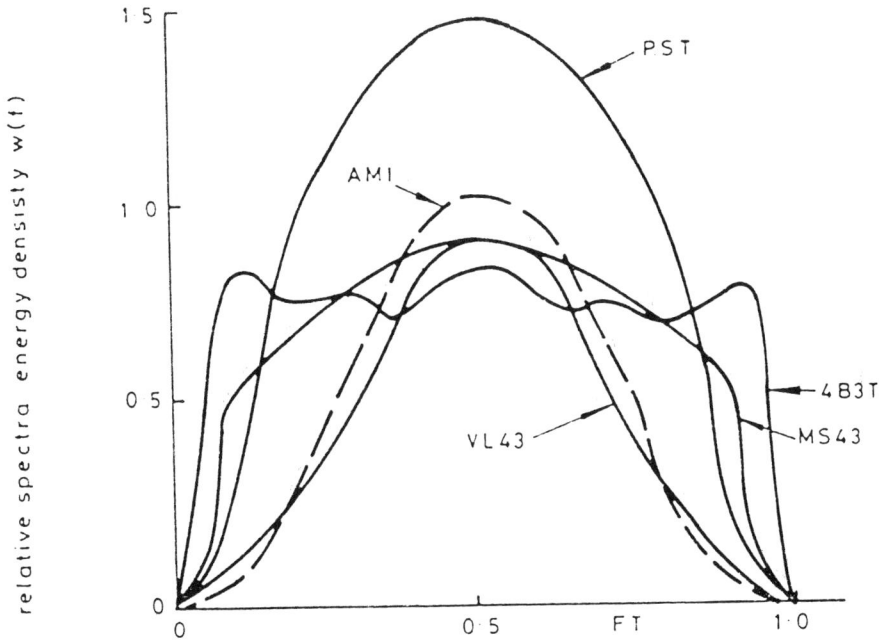

Fig.3.4 - Line code power spectra for alphabetic ternary codes.

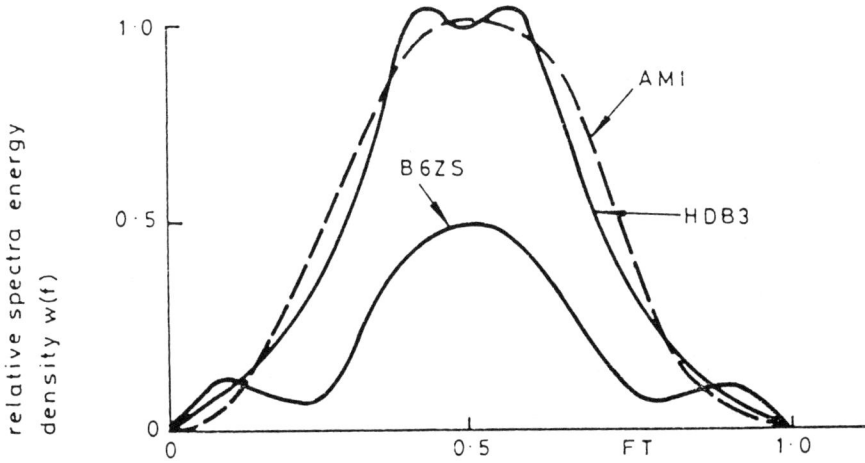

Fig.3.6 - Line code power spectra for non-alphabetic ternary codes.

4B3T-type codes. Two of these are the MS-43 code and the VL-43 code. Both of these codes have a more complex arrangement for mode alternation than the basic 4B3T code described above. The average power spectra for these two codes are also given in Fig.3.4.

NON-ALPHABETIC TERNARY CODES

In the non-alphabetic codes, long runs of zeros which may occur in conventional AMI coding are broken up by the substitution of pulses or groups of pulses which violate the AMI alternating pulse polarity rule. There are a number of ways this may be carried out, the most widely used method being the code known as HDB3 ('high density bipolar' with maximum of three consecutive zeros). HDB3 is a modification of AMI where, if more than three consecutive zeros occur, a 'violation' pulse is substituted for the fourth zero. The first violation pulse is selected so that it indeed violates the alternate mark inversion rule and is thus readily identifiable as representing binary zero rather than binary one. Subsequent violation pulses simply alternate in polarity from the first violation pulse to maintain low code disparity. This means, however, that some violation pulse substitutions are not identifiable from genuine marks. To avoid this confusion, any violation pulse which is of opposite polarity to the preceding mark pulse (genuine or a violation) is forced into violation by the insertion of a 'parity' pulse substituted for the first zero immediately following the preceding mark. The next genuine mark following a parity pulse is made of opposite polarity to the parity pulse, irrespective of the polarity of the previous genuine mark. In this way, unique decoding is possible. The procedure is probably more easily understood by considering a specific example. Consider the bit sequence given in Fig.3.5. The first violation pulse V_1 occurs in place of the fourth zero following the first mark pulse. It is of the same polarity as the initial mark. The second violation pulse V_2 occurs in place of the fourth zero in the next run of zeros and is of opposite polarity to the previous violation pulse. However, it does not violate the inversion rule with respect to the preceding mark pulse. Parity pulse P_1 is therefore inserted in place of the first

Binary digits   01 00000 101 000010 1 1001 100000

AMI

HDB3

V₁   P₁ V₂   V₃

(labels: V_1 P_1 V_2 V_3)

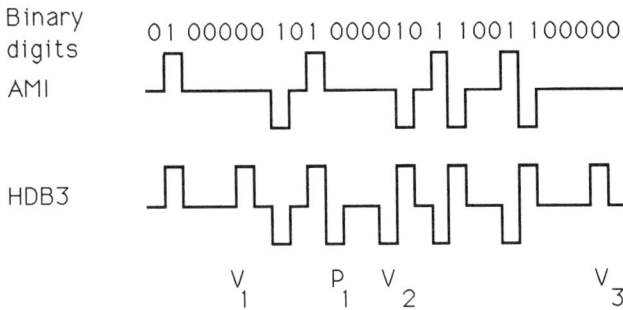

Fig.3.5 - HDB3 code.

zero in the run of zeros. The polarity of this pulse is chosen to cause violation by V_2. Obviously, on receipt, P_1 will first be considered as a mark. However, on detection of the violation pulse V_2, it will be clear that P_1 must have been a parity pulse and should therefore be interpreted as a zero. The next mark following the parity pulse is of opposite polarity to the parity pulse, the parity pulses being regarded as marks as far as the AMI rule is concerned, even though they in fact represent a zero value in the data sequence. Thus, following the parity pulse P_1 in Fig.3.5, the marks are of opposite polarity to what they would have been had conventional AMI code have been used. Finally, violation pulse V_3 occurs in place of the fourth zero in the third sequence of zeros. This pulse is of opposite polarity to V_2 and violates the alternate mark inversion rule with respect to the preceding mark pulse. No parity pulse is therefore necessary.

The average power spectrum for HDB3 is given in Fig.3.6, together with that of an alternative code known as B6ZS ('bipolar with six zeros substitution'). The B6ZS code is similar to HDB3, where any run of six consecutive zeros is replaced by a code group of pulses which can be identified at the receiver because some of the substituted pulses violate the basic AMI rule.

MULTILEVEL LINE CODES

Codes can also be designed using more than three pulse amplitude levels. For example, the quarternary (four-level) code 2B1Q takes pairs of bits from the binary input sequence and converts them into pulses with amplitudes -3, -1, +1 and +3 corresponding to the binary pairs 01, 00, 10 and 11 respectively. This procedure can be extended by taking n bits at a time and converting them into an m-ary signal where $m = 2^n$. The main disadvantage of the multilevel codes is that the greater the number of levels, the more vulnerable the code becomes to noise and interference from external sources such as crosstalk, impulsive noise and radio pick-up.

Error-detecting and correcting codes

INTRODUCTION

Unfortunately, however well we have designed our channel modulation or line-coding, no communication channel will be perfect. It is not possible to overcome the effects of noise and other channel impairments so that the received data is entirely error-free. We can do our best to minimise the possibility of such errors but, if we transmit data at a finite rate, then we have to accept the possibility that some errors will occur at some time during transmission. Generally the faster we try to transmit data over a given channel, the greater will be the proportion of bits in error. We therefore have to make a choice based on a compromise between a high rate of data trasnsmission and a very low proportion of bits in error. What this choice will be will depend on the nature of the data being transmitted. Digital video or speech signals require comparatively high data rates. However, the occasional error in transmission will have little subjective effect on the received signal. For encoded data processing information, such as that for transfer of financial transactions, the rate of transmission required is comparatively low, since relatively few bits are needed for a complete transmission. The integrity of the transmission, however, is of the utmost importance, since an error in a single data bit could lead to a change of several orders of magnitude in the size of the sum concerned, with possible disastrous consequences.

By using some of the transmitted bits as check digits, it is possible to provide some error detection, or even error correction, capability. Again, it is not possible to protect against the occurrence of every error. However, it is possible to provide protection to detect and, if necessary to correct, to any desired degree of accuracy, provided some finite, even if very small, probability of undetected error is acceptable. The proportion of transmitted bits that have to be used as check bits depends on the degree of error protection required. Transmission totally free from undetected error would require every bit transmitted to be a check digit, leaving no bits available for the transmission of actual data. Thus it is a practical impossibility to have transmission that is totally free of undetected error.

Those bits in the transmitted data stream that do not carry actual information are usually referred to as redundant bits. The check bits in error-detecting and error-correcting codes are therefore technically redundant bits, though, of course, they perform an invaluable function in the process of data transmission. It is useful to have a measure of the proportion of the bits in transmission which carry actual information. Thus we can define a code efficiency as the actual rate of information transmission, sometimes called data throughput, as a proportion of the actual rate of transmission of binary digits over the transmission medium, the line transmission bit-rate. Thus

$$\text{Efficiency} = \frac{\text{Data throughput}}{\text{Line transmission bit-rate.}}$$

In fact it is more common to talk in terms of the proportion of redundant bits in the data transmitted. Since all bits not carrying information may be regarded as redundant, we can define

$$\text{Redundancy} = 1 - \frac{\text{Data throughput}}{\text{Line tranmission bit-rate.}}$$

It is usual to express both effiency and redundancy as percentages, whence the values given above are multiplied by 100%.

Although error-correcting codes would appear, on the face of it, to be very attractive, they do, unfortunately, require considerably more redundancy than an error-detecting code of the same power. Often it is sufficient to know that the transmission has been in error. The message can then be ignored or a retransmission requested. The correction of errors by detection and retransmission is referred to as ARQ. We shall come back to this procedure later, when we have had an opportunity to look in detail at some codes which enable errors to be corrected without the need of retransmission. These codes are known as forward error-correcting codes. But first, we shall look at the simplest form of error-detection, the use of parity check bits.

ERROR DETECTION BY PARITY

The simple single parity check code enables all single errors in blocks of data bits to be detected, but it will not detect the occurrence of two errors in a block. However, by suitable choice of block size we can ensure that double errors are sufficiently unlikely to occur that the vast majority of errors in transmission are detected. We shall discuss how to choose a suitable block size later, but first we must consider the actual operation of the single parity check. The transmitted data is divided into suitable sized blocks and a single parity bit is added to each block. The additional bit is chosen so that there is either always an even number of 1 bits per block, known as even parity, or an odd number of 1 bits per block, known as odd parity. An example of even parity is given in Fig.4.1.

Block Code	Even parity
1 0 1 1 0 1 0 1	1
0 0 0 1 1 0 1 1	0

Fig.4.1 - Example of even parity.

On receipt, the parity of the block is checked and any violation of the parity rule will indicate an error somewhere in the block. Whether a 1 has been read as a 0, or a 0 as a 1, in either case the parity check will fail. Double errors will go undetected because changing any two bits in the block will lead to the correct parity being indicated on parity check at the receiver. The smaller the block size, the less chance of there being a double error. However, the smaller the block the greater the redundancy. We therefore need to choose a block size to give just the right amount of protection for the particular use envisaged. If we know the bit error probability in the basic transmitted data stream without error detection (p_t) and the maximum acceptable probability of an undetected error (p_e), we can determine the required block size as follows:

Let n = block size, then probability of a single bit in error in a block of size n = np_t and probability of two bits in error in a block of size n

$$= \frac{n(n-1)}{2} \, p_t^2.(1 - p_t)^{n-2}$$

In all practical situations p_t will be sufficiently small that we can safely neglect all triple and higher order errors per block and also assume that the term $(1 - p_t)^{n-2}$ is approximately equal to 1. Thus, if we detect all single errors, we can assume that practically all the remaining errors will be of the order of 2 bits per block. Thus, when the blocks with single errors have been eliminated, the remaining errors will give an approximate overall bit error probability of

$$\frac{n(n-1) \, p_t^2 \times 1 \times 2}{2 \quad\quad n} = (n-1) \, p_t^2 \le p_e \qquad\qquad (4.1)$$

$$\therefore \; n \le \frac{p_e}{p_t^2} + 1$$

In fact the approximation is even better than would appear at first sight because all triple and higher odd order errors will be detected, whereas all even order errors will go undetected rather than all errors of order greater than 1 going undetected.

In practice it is more usual to speak of bit error-rates rather than probability of bit error. This presents no difficulty, since an error-rate of 1 in 10^x is equivalent to a probability of error of 10^{-x}. For example, an error-rate of 1 in 10^3 (i.e. 1 in 1000) is equivalent to a probability of error of 0.001 (i.e. 10^{-3}). Thus if we have a transmission system with a basic transmission error-rate of 1 in 10^4 and our acceptable undetected error-rate is 1 in 10^6, then our block size n is given by:

$$n \le \frac{10^{-6}}{10^{-8}} + 1 = 101$$

Note n must be integer and that one of the bits in the block will be a parity bit. Thus, for any transmission to be possible, n must be ≥ 2, thus p_e/p_t^2 must be ≥ 1. Thus it is impossible to provide protection to give p_e, the undetected error-rate, greater than p_t^2, where p_t is the probability of error in transmission. Thus, with the transmission error-rate of 1 in 10^4 given above, it is impossible, parity check, to obtain an undetected error-rate of better than 1 in 10^8, and this would require a redundancy of 50% (i.e. 2 bits per block, one a data bit and the other a parity check on that bit)

ERROR CORRECTION BY BLOCK PARITY

The concept of parity checking can be extended to detect and correct all single errors in a data block.   The data block is arranged in rectangular matrix form as shown in Fig.4.2.

a	b	c	d	P1
e	f	g	h	P2
i	j	k	l	P3

P7	P6	P5	P4

Fig.4.2. - Block parity for single error correction.

Parity bits are then provided for each row and each column in the matrix. A change in any single bit will now cause the failure of two parity checks and the position of the parity failures will enable the erroneous data bit to be located and hence corrected.   Since the bit can only have one of two states, correction of an erroneous bit simply involves a reversal of the state of that particular bit. An erroneous parity bit, and these are just as vulnerable as the data bits, will be indicated by one parity failure only.

Multiple errors, of course, will lead to meaningless or even misleading indications of parity failure.   However, since the probability of a single error is so much greater than that of a double error, and higher order errors are even less probable, the code can be used effectively to substantially reduce the error-rate, provided the block size is chosen small enough.   Note, however, that the redundancy increases rapidly with reduction in block size and that the redundancy required is considerably greater than that required for single error detection only.

HAMMING DISTANCE

It is time we looked a little closer at the theory of error-detecting and error-correcting codes in order to be able to specify the code capability and to design efficient coding techniques. To simplify our terminology we shall use the concept of a code-word. A code-word is a group of binary digits taken together to form a recognisable coding entity. Thus a data block, together with the added redundant bits, may be regarded as a code-word. Hamming distance can then be defined as the number of corresponding bits in two code-words from a code-word group that are different in state. Thus the Hamming distance between the two words given below is 3.

$$0 \quad 0 \quad 1 \quad 0 \quad 1 \quad 1 \quad 0 \quad 1$$
$$X \qquad\qquad\qquad X \qquad X$$
$$1 \quad 0 \quad 1 \quad 0 \quad 0 \quad 1 \quad 1 \quad 1$$

Similarly, the distance between the two following words will be 4.

$$0 \quad 0 \quad 0 \quad 0 \quad 1 \quad 1 \quad 1 \quad 1$$
$$\qquad\quad X \quad X \quad X \quad X$$
$$0 \quad 0 \quad 1 \quad 1 \quad 0 \quad 0 \quad 1 \quad 1$$

From the concept of Hamming distance we can deduce the following rules:

(a) If the minimum distance between any two words in a set of code-words is 1, then a single error is likely to change the word into another word in the set and error detection is thus impossible.

(b) If the minimum distance between any two words in a set of code-words is 2, then it is possible to detect all single errors since at least two errors are needed to alter any word into another in the set.

(c) If the minimum distance between any two words in a set of code-words is 3, then it is possible to correct all single errors since a single error will still leave the word at least two bits different from any other word in the set. It is therefore possible to detemine which word was sent since the correct word will be the only one which has a distance 1 from the received word. Unfortunately, a double error is likely to lead to a third error being produced and the three errors passed on undetected, since two errors can result in a received word which differs in only one position from another word in the set.   This would thus be interpreted as a single error which would be incorrectly interpreted as a code-word of distance 3 from the one transmitted.   Code-words with a distance of 3 can be used to detect all single and double errors, providing single errors are not to be corrected.

(d)   With a minimum distance of 4, it is possible to correct single errors and detect double errors at the same time.   To correct both single and double errors we need a minimum distance of 5 between code-words. It can be shown that to correct up to k errors per code-word will require a Hamming distance of $D = 2k + 1$.

It is surprising how many redundant bits are required to obtain a Hamming distance of any significance. For example, it is only possible to select 4 code-words of 5 bit length having a Hamming distance of 3, that is, sufficient distance to carry out single error correction.   The full set of words and their implication, for a particular selection of 4 words of 5 bits, is given in Fig.4.3.

$$
\left.
\begin{array}{l}
00000 \\
10011 \\
11100 \\
01111
\end{array}
\right\}
\quad
\begin{array}{l}
\text{These are not the only set of} \\
\text{four we could have chosen.}
\end{array}
$$

00000	10011	11100	01111	Code-word
00001	10010	11101	01110	
00010	10001	11110	01101	
00100	10111	11000	01011	Single bit errors
01000	11011	10100	00111	
10000	00011	01100	11111	

These combinations occur only with two errors:

00101	00110	01001	01010
11010	11001	10110	10101

Fig.4.3 - Five bit code words with distance three.

HAMMING CODES

It is possible to devise effective single-error-correcting codes which are more efficient than the block parity check codes in that they require fewer bits to achieve the same degree of error correction.   It can be shown that optimum use of redundancy for single error correction requires n bits of a block size N to be parity bits, where $n = \log_2(N+1)$.   Since it is impossible to have fractional bits, n must be rounded up to the nearest integer.   The most efficient block sizes are those that require no rounding up, that is, where $N = 2^n - 1$, n integer.   The next bit to be added to a block of this size will have of necessity to be a parity check.   In fact a systematic arrangement for such a code is for the bits in positions 2^n, $n = 0, 1, 2, 3,$ . . . . . ., to be allocated for parity checking.   A code arranged on this basis is generally referred to as a Hamming code.   An example of a Hamming code for N = 7, n = 3, is given in Table 4.1.   It will be evident from the table how the code can be extended for any required block size.   The position of the error is indicated by parity check failures as shown in the table.   The number of the position is given directly in binary form by entering 1 for a failure and 0 for a pass in the error check table.   Errors are corrected by bit reversal.   Note that errors in the parity bits are signified by a single indicated error in the check table.

It will now be evident why it was only possible to select four code-words with a mimimum distance 3 from the set of 5-bit code-words.   In this case bits 1, 2 and 4 must be parity check bits, leaving only bits 3 and 5 for data.   This permits only four data combinations.   The four words selected in the example given in Fig. 4.3 are in fact those given by a 5-bit Hamming code selection.

It is, of course, not necessary that the bits be transmitted in the strict sequence of the coding rule.   An alternative would be to transmit the data bits first, followed by the parity checks.   However, the rules for determining the value of the parity bits and the position of the detected errors must be based on the basic code structure for satisfactory operation.

The larger the block size, the lower the redundancy, since the parity bits occur more densely at the beginning of the code word.   As with the error-correcting code, the more powerful the error-correcting requirement, the smaller the block size must be, with a corresponding greater redundancy.   We can calculate the block

Table 4.1 - Hamming code for N = 7, n = 3

	K_1	K_2	Data	K_3		Data	
Data	1	2	3	4	5	6	7
0	0	0	0	0	0	0	0
1	1	1	0	1	0	0	1
2	0	1	0	1	0	1	0
3	1	0	0	0	0	1	1
4	1	0	0	1	1	0	0
5	0	1	0	0	1	0	1
6	1	1	0	0	1	1	0
7	0	0	0	1	1	1	1
8	1	1	1	0	0	0	0
9	0	0	1	1	0	0	1
10	1	0	1	1	0	1	0
11	0	1	1	0	0	1	1
12	0	1	1	1	1	0	0
13	1	0	1	0	1	0	1
14	0	0	1	0	1	1	0
15	1	1	1	1	1	1	1

K_1 is even parity on positions 1, 3, 5, 7.
K_2 is even parity on positions 2, 3, 6, 7.
K_3 is even parity on positions 4, 5, 6, 7.
Data is given in binary form in positions 3, 5, 6, 7.
Single errors cause failure of parity checks thus:
(1 = failure, 0 = check passed)

	K_3	K_2	K_1
No error	0	0	0
Error in position 1	0	0	1
Error in position 2	0	1	0
Error in position 3	0	1	1
Error in position 4	1	0	0
Error in position 5	1	0	1
Error in position 6	1	1	0
Error in position 7	1	1	1

size required in a way similar to that used for the error-detecting code. In this case, rather than eliminate the blocks with the single errors, we will in fact correct these errors. In the case of double errors, we have another factor to consider. Since our code has been designed optimally to have a Hamming distance of three between each code word, any word with two errors will only be distance one from another code word. It will therefore be assumed that the word transmitted was that word and that it had been received with a single error. It will therefore be erroneously 'corrected' to give a word distance three from that transmitted, that is, it will convert a double error into a triple error. Thus the last term in our formula for the overall bit-error probability after correction of single errors will differ from that given in (4.1). Hence the overall bit-error probability after correction of single errors is given by

$$\frac{p(n-1)}{2} \cdot p_t^2 \times \frac{1}{n} \times 3$$

$$= \quad \frac{2(n-1)}{3} p_t^2 \leq p_e$$

$$\therefore n \leq \frac{2p_e}{3p_t^2} + 1 \qquad\qquad (4.2)$$

Thus if the basic transmission error-rate is 1 in 10^4 and an acceptable error-rate after correction of single errors is 1 in 10^6, then our block size n is given by

$$n \leq \frac{2}{3} \times \frac{10^{-6}}{10^{-8}} + 1$$

$$\leq 67.$$

With a block size of 67, the parity bits will occupy positions 1, 2, 4, 8, 16, 32 and 64. There will thus be 7 parity bits and 60 information bits in each block. The code efficiency is therefore 60/67 x 100 = 89.6%. We could, of course, choose a block of smaller size than 67, in which case the code would have a rather better error-correcting performance. If we choose a block size of 63, then we would have only 6 parity bits, in positions 1, 2, 4, 8, 16 and 32. We will then have 57 information bits, giving an efficiency of 57/63 x 100 = 90.5%. Note that this is in fact more efficient than a block size of 67, a warning that it is not always prudent to chose the largest block size given by our formula (4.2). A parity bit near the end of the code word is an indication that we should look carefully at the possibility of curtailing the word length to eliminate this final parity bit.

ALGEBRAIC CODES

The algebraic codes present a more general approach to errror-correcting codes and include the Hamming code as a special case. Let us assume, as before, that our set of code-words consists of N digits, n of these digits being parity check digits. Thus m = N - n digits actually carry information. Although with N-digit words it is possible to select 2^N different code-words, in fact only 2^m words are used in the code-word set. We can express the rule used for the selection of the subset of code-words used using Boolean matrix algebra notation. The words are chosen to satisfy the equation [H]T' = 0, where T' is the N column vector which is the transpose of T, the N row vector representing the selected code word and [H] is an n x N matrix where each column is unique and non-zero. Thus, for example, the Hamming code for N = 7, n = 3, is generated using the matrix

$$[H] = \begin{bmatrix} 1 & 0 & 1 & 0 & 1 & 0 & 1 \\ 0 & 1 & 1 & 0 & 0 & 1 & 1 \\ 0 & 0 & 0 & 1 & 1 & 1 & 1 \end{bmatrix}$$

It is usual, though not essential, to take the positions represented by the columns containing only a single 1 as the parity check digits in the code-words. Thus for the Hamming code for N = 7, the check digits are in the first, second and fourth positions. It is a simple matter to re-order the matrix so that the check digits occur after the information-carrying digits. For example:

$$[H] = \begin{bmatrix} 1 & 1 & 0 & 1 & 1 & 0 & 0 \\ 1 & 0 & 1 & 1 & 0 & 1 & 0 \\ 0 & 1 & 1 & 1 & 0 & 0 & 1 \end{bmatrix}$$

When a code-word is received, the receiver determines the product of the received code-word with the matrix [H]. Since for all acceptable code words the product $[H]T' = 0$, if the product formed at the receiver is other than zero we know that at least a single error must have occurred in transmission.

If T is the row vector representing the transmitted word and R is the row vector representing the received word, then we can define an error vector E which contains a 1 in each position in which an error has occurred. Then $R = T + E$ and hence, by simple transpositions into column vectors, $R' = T' + E'$, where the addition is Boolean (modulo-2).

Now the product at the receiver $[H]R' = [H](T' + E')$

$$= [H]T' + [H]E'$$

However, by definition $[H]T' = 0$, hence $[H]R' = [H]E'$.

Thus our multiplication operation at the receiver gives us directly the value $[H]E'$, usually referred to as the code syndrome. We can then identify the position of a single error in the received code word by selecting the position of the column in the matrix H which corresponds with the syndrome $[H]E'$. Since the digits in the received message have only two possible states, any indicated error can easily be corrected by simply reversing the state of the digit in question. It will now be clear why each column in the matrix [H] needs to be unique and non-zero. If it were zero, then it would be indistiguishable from the 'all correct' indication.

Let us take an example. If we assume that the word 1 1 0 1 0 0 1 from the Hamming code set was transmitted but was received as 1 1 0 1 1 0 1, when the receiver product is formed we get

$$[H]R' = \begin{bmatrix} 1 & 0 & 1 & 0 & 1 & 0 & 1 \\ 0 & 1 & 1 & 0 & 0 & 1 & 1 \\ 0 & 0 & 0 & 1 & 1 & 1 & 1 \end{bmatrix} \cdot \begin{bmatrix} 1 \\ 1 \\ 0 \\ 1 \\ 1 \\ 0 \\ 1 \end{bmatrix} = \begin{bmatrix} 1 \\ 0 \\ 1 \end{bmatrix}$$

The syndrome is seen to be equal to the fifth column of the matrix [H], thus indicating an error in the fifth digit of the recived code-word. Inversion of the appropriate digit is all that is necessary to correct the error. The concept of algebraic codes can be extended to the correction of multiple errors but further consideration of these possibilities is beyond the scope of this book.

CYCLIC REDUNDANCY CHECK CODES

The identifying feature of a cyclic code is the property that a cyclic, or end-about, shift of any code-word results in another code-word from the set. The attractiveness of the cyclic codes is that they can be implemented fairly easily using shift-register techniques. A code-word of length N with m information digits is referred to as an (N,m) cyclic code. The words of the code set are formed by Boolean division of a code word of length N, consisting of m information digits followed by n = N - m zeros, by a binary divisor of length n + 1. The remainder following the division is then inserted in place of the n zeros following the m information digits. Because of the complementary nature of modulo 2 division, the transmitted code-word will then be divisible without remainder by the initial divisor. Any remainder after so dividing a received code-word will indicate an error in transmission. A simple example in given in Fig.4.4.

The power of the code to detect and/or correct errors is determined by the relative magnitudes of the information and check fields m and n and also by the selection of the divisor. Unfortunately there are no simple rules for determining the best divisors for any particular circumstances. Thus anyone designing a cyclic redundancy check code must refer to the extensive literature on the subject.

A widely used cyclic redundancy code, specified in CCITT recommendation V41, is the (256, 240) code with the divisor 1 0 0 0 1 0 0 0 0 0 0 1 0 0 0 0 1. It is usual, and less confusing, to specify the divisor in the form of a 'characteristic polynomial'. The characteristic polynomial for the V41 divisor is

$$X^{16} + X^{12} + X^5 + 1.$$

```
                    Data
1 0 0 1  | 1 1 0 1 0 1 0 1 | 0 0 0
           1 0 0 1
           1 0 0 0
           1 0 0 1                    (n−1) zeros
             1 1 0 1
             1 0 0 1
               1 0 0   0
               1 0 0   1
                   1 0 0  ←  Remainder
                    Data
1 0 0 1  | 1 1 0 1 0 1 0 1 | 1 0 0
           1 0 0 1
           1 0 0 0                    Division is Modulo−2
           1 0 0 1
             1 1 0 1
             1 0 0 1
               1 0 0 1
               1 0 0 1
                   ←  No remainder
```

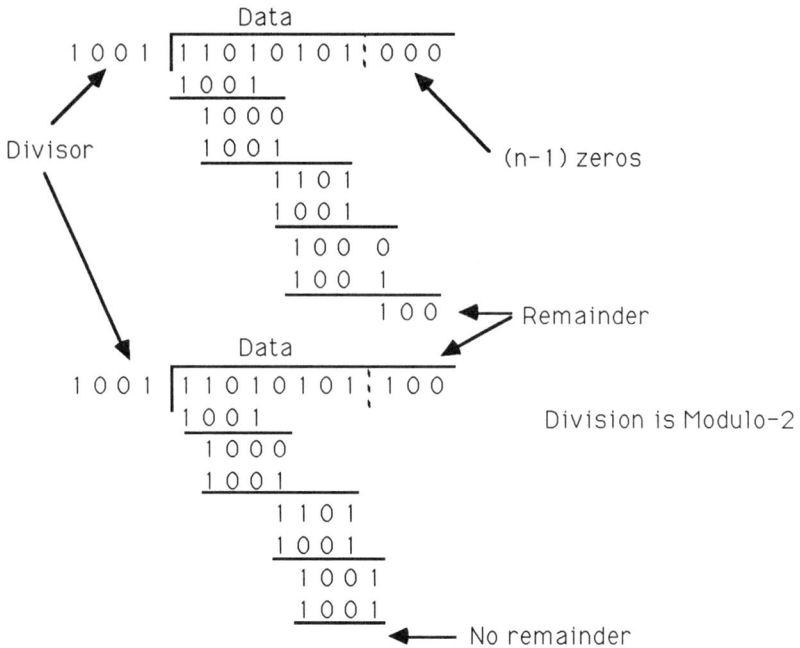

Fig.4.4 - Example of cyclic redundancy code generation.

The index to each term in the polynomial indicates the position of a 1 in the divisor, numbering the least significant position as 0. The V41 code will only permit error detection and is normally used in conjunction with ARQ (request repeat of blocks detected to be in error) operation. However, the divisor has been so chosen as to give a high degree of multiple error detection, especially errors occurring in short bursts.

CONVOLUTION CODES

All the codes described so far operate on a block basis and are most efficient in dealing with errors which occur at random. Unfortunately, in practice, errors frequently occur in bursts since noise impairments are often impulsive in nature rather than being in the form of additive, white, gaussian niose. The convolution codes are particularly useful for detecting and correcting burst errors. In the convolution codes, the data stream is not divided into blocks. Instead, parity checks are made on digits separated by several further digits and the check digits are inserted between the information digits elsewhere in the stream. The Hagelbarger code is a basic form of convolution code.

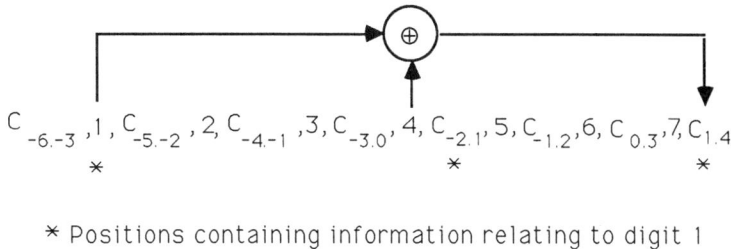

$$C_{-6,-3}, 1, C_{-5,-2}, 2, C_{-4,-1}, 3, C_{-3,0}, 4, C_{-2,1}, 5, C_{-1,2}, 6, C_{0,3}, 7, C_{1,4}$$

* Positions containing information relating to digit 1

Fig.4.5 - The Hagelbarger code.

THE HAGELBARGER CODE

In the Hagelbarger code alternate digits in the transmitted data stream are check digits formed by modulo-2 sum of the mth and nth preceding information digits. This means that information about a single digit is held in three places spread out in time according to the selection of the values of m and n. The redundancy of such a code is 50%. The Hagelbarger code is illustrated in Fig.4.5. Note that in this example m = 7 and n = 14. In this particular example up to six consecutive errors would be corrected, provided there are at least 19 error-free digits between bursts. If the information relating to a single digit is spread more widely in the digit stream, then larger bursts can be corrected but longer error-free runs between bursts are necessary for satisfactory error correction.

ERROR CORRECTION BY RE-TRANSMISSION (ARQ)

The error-correcting codes we have discussed give what is called 'forward error correction', that is, errors are corrected before the messages are passed to the receiver. The main disadvantage of forward error correction is the large amount of redundancy usually required for these codes. It is therefore often more convenient simply to detect errors and then request the re-transmission of any faulty blocks. This mode of operation is sometimes called ARQ. The practicability of doing this depends on the ability to transmit control information back to the sender and for the sender to store information until it has been acknowledged by the receiver. The process of acknowledgement is referred to as 'hand-shaking'. A disadvantage of ARQ is that, unless each block is stored at the receiver before being output to the terminal, it is not possible to have 'clean copy' output. The choice between forward error correction and ARQ depends on the availablity of a return channel, the economics of implementing the coding and decoding strategies, the transmission time requirements and the probability and acceptibility of errors in transmission.

Data networks.

INTRODUCTION.

So far we have only considered the problem of transmitting data over a link between two specific users. In fact we would rarely wish to restrict data communication to between a single pair of users, though this may be perfectly adequate for some applications. A much more common requirement is the ability to communicate with any one, or more, of a number of data terminals connected together to form a data network. The requirements for a data network are many and varied, depending on the particular application envisaged. We shall therefore look at data networks under a number of headings, some of which are important enough to merit a whole chapter of their own. However, in recent times a lot of attention has been given to the possibility of providing a set of general network requirements that will allow data terminals to be interconnected by the network in an unrestricted way. This concept of unrestricted interconnection is known as 'Open Systems Interconnection' (OSI). To achieve Open Systems Interconnection a hierarchical protocol structure is required that allows users of different equipment to obtain interworking over the network without their having to concern themselves with the detail of operation of each of the various levels of network function. Such a structure has been proposed by the International Standards Organisation (ISO) and is known as the ISO 7-layer protocol model for OSI. Before we look at networks in more detail it will be useful to take a quick look at the OSI model.

OSI PROTOCOL MODEL

The OSI model identifies seven levels or layers for the definition of protocols and interfaces for open systems interconnection. The model is illustrated in Fig.5.1.

At the lowest level, level 1, physical parameters for signals are defined simply to enable signals to be transferred over the physical connection. This layer, the

Layer	Level		Level
Application	7	←·······→	7
Presentation	6	←·······→	6
Session	5	←·······→	5
Transport	4	←·······→	4
Network	3	←·······→	3
Link	2	←·······→	2
Physical	1	←·······→	1
	Physical Connection		

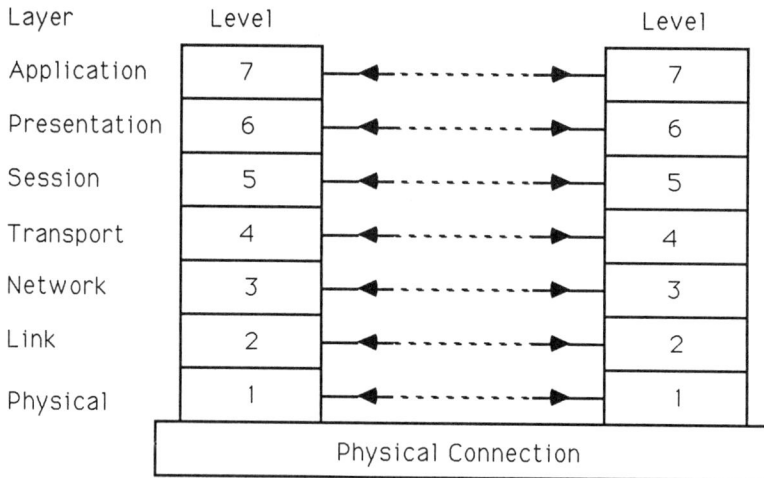

Fig. 5.1 - The ISO 7-layer model for open systems interconnection.

Physical Layer, consists of specifications for the line code, transmission rate, signal voltage levels, physical connectors and other parameters to enable satisfactory transfer of streams of digits over a simple single connection path. At this level, no significance is attached to any single digit, it is concerned only with the efficient transfer of data across the physical connection.

The second layer, the Link Layer, is concerned with the establishment of a disciplined and reliable data link across the physical link. At the physical level there is an inherent degree of unreliability in that there is no knowing whether errors have occured in the transfer of data. Thus one of the major functions of the Link Level is to provide error detecting and/or correcting facilities. This in itself may require the division of the data stream into blocks so as to identify the field over which any error-detecting code operates. Alternatively, block delimiters may be necessary for synchronisation purposes. Although various digits now perform specific functions, nevertheless the basic transparency of the data link is maintained in the bits allocated to the data field in the Link protocol.

A data network comprises a number of nodes interconnected by various data links. The third layer in the OSI model is concerned with network operation and is known as the Network Layer. At this level addresses are required to specify the links to be used to interconnect the appropriate terminal nodes. This may specify logical links rather than specific physical paths, since the same physical path may not necessarily be used for successive packets of the same message transaction. Control and acknowledgement fields are also provided to ensure that data communication is correctly established between the appropriate network nodes. The network control should be independent both of the Link Level of control and the higher order levels of protocol.

The three layers so far considered are concerned only with the communications network and are thus properly the concern of the communications engineer. The fourth layer, the Transport Layer, takes into account the nature of the terminal equipment and is concerned with establishing a transport service suited to the needs of this equipment. It must thus select a link through the network which operates at a data rate and quality appropriate to the needs of the terminals involved in the communication operation, thus relieving the user from concerning himself with the detail of the mechanism of data transfer through the network. We are thus beginning to depart from the basic task of providing a communication path through the network.

The next three layers, layers 5 to 7, are task-oriented and have to do with the operations performed by the data terminal equipment rather than with the network. The Session Layer is concerned with setting up and maintaining an operational session between terminals. It can thus be identified basically with the operation of 'signing on' the computer to begin the operation of the desired task and 'signing off' to signify the completion of the task.

The Presentation Layer is concerned with the format in which data is to be presented to the terminals and resolves differences in representation of information used by the application task. Each task can thus communicate without knowing the representation of information (e.g. data code) used by a different task. The purpose of this layer is to make the network machine-independent.

The Application Layer defines the nature of the task to be performed. It provides the actual user information processing function and programs for application processes in the real world, for example, airline booking, banking, electronic mail, word-processing etc. These three higher order layers are mainly concerned with the organisation of the terminal software and are not directly the concern of the communications engineer. The Transport Layer is the layer which links the communication processes to these software-oriented protocols.

The basic philosophy of the 7-layer model is that each layer may be defined independently of every other layer. Thus from the user point of view, interchange takes effect across each layer as shown by the broken line connections in the diagram. In fact each operation passes down through the layers of the model until data interchange is effected through the physical connection.

We shall now look in a little more detail at some specific network strategies.

DATA NETWORKS BASED ON PSTN

Some data networks, for example those associated with computer bureaux, consist of a large number of terminals which require only occasional connection to the central computer facility. For such an application the switched telephone network provides the best method of connection. The DATEL 600 service is the service most used by computer bureaux. This offers a 1200 bits/s service, with a fall-back facility to 600 bits/s for poor quality circuits, and a return channel operating at 75 bits/s. Such a service is ideal for reception of information using Visual Display Units (VDUs), which normally operate at 600/1200 bits/s, together with keyboard sending, which uses 75 bits/s for normal typing speeds of up to 10 characters per second. Although direct connection to the network using modems is preferred, it is possible to obtain this service via almost any telephone handset, using a portable terminal connected by means of an acoustic coupler. This couples the terminal directly to the hand-set by the use of a pair of audio tones to denote the data conditions 0 and 1.

For higher speeds of operation it is possible to lease special data-quality lines. These lines are part of the public telephone network but are selected to provide maximum isolation from sources of cross-talk and are patched at the exchange to avoid the need to pass through the switching equipment. The lines are thus dedicated to a particular user for considerable periods of time. They are therefore most useful when they form part of a large and complex computer network facility. Data rates available on data-quality leased lines are 2400 bits/s, 4800 bits/s and, under suitable circumstances, 9600 bits/s.

The earliest computer networks were designed to enable several terminals to access the same central computer. There were two main uses for such a facility. First, in the 1960's, computers were physically large and comparatively expensive. It was therefore desirable for a number of users to be able to make use of a single main-frame computer by access from remote terminals. Secondly, a number of applications were beginning to emerge where a number of geographically separate users required access to a common shared data-base. Amongst the earliest of these were the airline seat reservation service networks, the first of which began operation in the United States in 1961. Other early users of computer networks were the banks, who used them to enable branches to obtain direct access to centrally stored account information and to remotely update this information as transactions took place.

To allow terminals to communicate with a central computer in turn, it was necessary to establish some form of access protocol. These early networks were operated on a "polled" strategy, where the central computer invites the various data terminals to communicate in turn according to some pre-determined rule. There are basically two types of polling, "roll-call" polling and "hub" polling. In roll-call polling the terminals are normally in the "listening" mode waiting to receive signals broadcast from the central computer. Each broadcast message includes a terminal address field. On recognising its address, a terminal becomes active, either to receive a message or to respond to an invitation to transmit. If the terminal has no data to transmit when it receives an invitation, it simply responds with an indication to this effect. The order in which terminals are polled is thus entirely in the control of the central computer. It is not a pre-requisite that terminals be polled sequentially. Some terminals may be given priority by more frequent entries in the roll-call table. The roll-call list can be dynamically re-arranged should priority requirements change. The disadvantage of roll-call polling is that, for very wide area networks, there could be significant delay in consecutive interrogations due to propagation delays in the network. This can be reduced by the use of hub polling. (See Figs.5.2 and 5.3).

Hub polling differs from roll-call polling in that the interrogation, instead of being initiated by the central computer, is initiated by the preceding terminal on the loop. When a terminal has completed its transaction, or if it has no message to send in response to the invitation, it passes on the polling invitation directly to the next

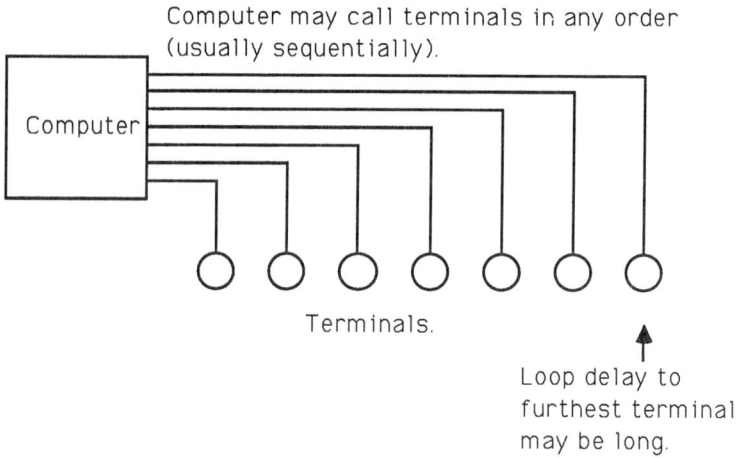

Computer may call terminals in any order
(usually sequentially).

Computer

Terminals.

Loop delay to
furthest terminal
may be long.

Fig.5.2. - Roll-call polling.

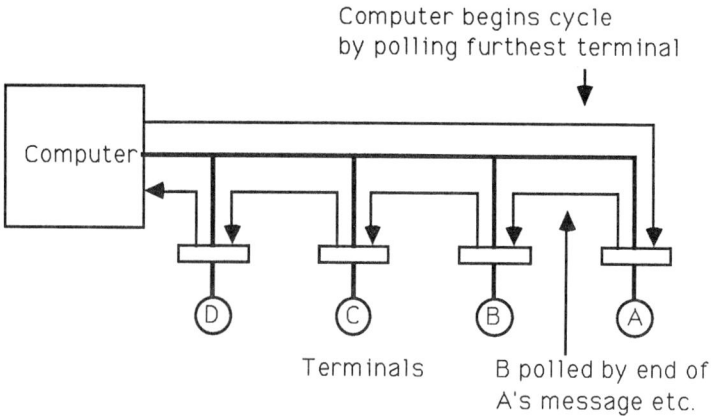

Computer begins cycle
by polling furthest terminal

Computer

D   C   B   A

Terminals   B polled by end of
A's message etc.

Fig.5.3. - Hub polling.

terminal in the sequence. On long-distance networks, the time required to pass the
polling information can be greatly reduced by this means. The penalty for this is
more equipment at the terminal to provide the extra intelligence necessary to initiate
the polling. It is also more difficult to arrange for priority users and to modify the
polling sequence than it is for roll-call polling.

Most modern applications for data networks, however, require much higher
bit-rates than can be obtained over the public switched telephone network. In any
case, the pattern of data traffic is vastly different to that of normal telephone traffic

and can therefore seriously interfere with the network operation, where equipment is provided so as to satisfy the requirements for normal telephone demands. Specifically data networks have therefore been provided, which are designed to meet the special requirements imposed by the traffic demands of data communication equipment. These networks can be divided into two classes, Local Area Networks (LANs) and Wide Area Networks (WANs).

LOCAL AREA NETWORKS

Much of the requirement for data transmission is for systems confined within the boundaries of a large building or campus. The whole network operates within a private area and there is no requirement for public data transmission facilities provided by one of the companies licensed to provide public data network services. They are therefore normally privately controlled and can thus be designed to meet the special needs of the user concerned. Such a facility is generally designated a Local Area Network (LAN). We shall look at various types of LAN in some detail in Chapter 7.

WIDE AREA NETWORKS

Wide area networks (WANs) are networks in which the users are not confined to a single location but are located at various sites within a region or nationally, or even internationally. The requirements of Wide Area Networks are many and varied and depend, to a large degree, on the nature of the application. Some Wide Area Networks are still based on the telephone network, using the telephone switching facilities and the DATEL services to provide digital transmission. This service has the advantage that the telephone network is accessible in almost every part of the world and its very ubiquitousness makes it attractive for many applications. However, as we have already seen, it is extremely limited on the data rates it can offer for data transfer applications.   The fact that telephony itself is rapidly becoming a digitally transmitted and digitally switched service means that direct access to the digital telephone facilities provides a useful way of extending the use of the telephone network for digital transmission purposes.   The details of data services available as a result of the conversion of the telephone network to digital operation are described the following section. Unfortunately, at the present time digital telephony has not yet been provided universally, even within the UK. However, plans are under way which should mean that virtually the whole of the telephone network in the UK will be operating entirely digitally by the turn of the century. There will then be no need to treat data and speech as separate services and we can expect to see the coming to maturity of the proposed Integrated Services Digital Network (ISDN). This is such an important development that the proposals, which are currently being implemented in some areas where digital (System X) telephone exchanges have already been installed, are discussed in detail in the final chapter of this book. It is almost certain that the first few years of the 21st century will see ISDN as the back-bone to international communication for not only speech and data but for other digital services such as video and facimile.

KILOSTREAM AND MEGASTREAM

Kilostream and Megastream services have become available as a direct result of the progressive digitisation of the UK telephone network. To understand why these services are available, and to understand their limitations, we need to look at the reasons why it is considered desirable to send speech signals in digital form and at the way this process is carried out in practice.

When we transmit an analogue speech signal over a channel which has a finite transmission loss and is subject to noise impairment, and all channels have these deficiencies to some degree, then, as the length of the transmission path is increased, the received signal-to-noise ratio progressively decreases. Ultimately the signal can become completely masked by the additive noise. However, if we sample our original signal at a suitable rate and represent the sample amplitude digitally, using an appropriate number of binary digits to represent the sample with adequate enough precision, then we can represent our signal as a sequence of binary digits. We can then reconstruct our orginal analogue signal at the receiver from the sample amplitudes received in digital form. The process of conversion from an analogue to digital signal at the sender is known as analogue-to-digital conversion (ADC) and the process of reconstruction at the receiver is known as digital-to-analogue conversion (DAC). We shall, of course, require a greater channel bandwidth to transmit our train of digits than we would have required for our original analogue signal. However, we now only have to be able to recognise the presence, or polarity, of pulses in a pulse train. This we can do with reasonable accuracy at levels of noise which would certainly have completely masked our original analogue signal. What is more, instead of intermediate amplifiers, which increase the noise as well as the signal, we can install regenerators along the line. These regenerate the pulse train entirely free of noise. We thus have a technique which will enable us to transmit signals over channels whivh would otherwise be useless because of the noise impairment of the signal.

In order to adequately represent a telephone speech signal using digital techniques, we need to sample at a rate of 8000 samples per second. Each sample then requires 8 bits to represent its amplitude to ensure sufficient precision to give no significant deterioration in the quality of the reconstructed signal. Note that 8 bits gives a range of 2^8 = 256 amplitude quantisation levels. In practice these are not uniformly spaced, greater spacing being used for the quantisation of large amplitudes than is used at the smaller amplitudes. This process is known as companding. The details of companding are not really relevant to our purposes here, suffice it to say that the idea is to make the error in quantisation, which gives rise to an effect known as quantisation noise, roughly proportional to the amplitude of the signal being subject to quantisation. Thus the signal-to-quantisation noise ratio remains roughly constant irrespective of the amplitude of the speech signal. This is important since speech signals vary very widely in amplitude, the ear adapting to compensate for this variation. This process of digitisation by sampling and quantisation is known as pulse-code-modulation (PCM). The basic digital transmission rate used to transmit a single speech signal using PCM is thus 8 x 8000 = 64 kbits/s.

Because ADC and DAC equipment has, until now, been relatively costly, it has not so far been practicable to provide each user with his own ADC and DAC. The connection from the user to the local exchange has therefore remained analogue and the conversion to and from PCM has taken place at the local exchange.

It is not usually economical in practice to use a separate electrical circuit for each individual connection from the local exchange into the junction and trunk networks.

Instead, several connections are "multiplexed" together so that they may use a single electrical circuit. The practice for PCM is to multiplex together thirty 64 kbits/s speech channels, together with two extra 64 kbits/s channels for synchronisation and signalling purposes at a digital transmission rate of 32 x 64 kbits/s = 2.048 Mbits/s. This 2.048 Mbits/s facility is referred to as "primary rate access". In fact several primary rate channels may be multiplexed together to give even higher digital transmission rates. These will not concern us here, but will be of importance when we discuss integrated services digital networks in the final chapter.

Provided some form of digital access connection can be made to the local exchange, there is no reason why a data user should not lease a basic PCM channel at a rate of 64 kbits/s for the transmission of data signals. The network is transparent to the 64 kbits/s signal and it is therefore of no importance to the network whether the signal represents speech using PCM or some other data signal. This service is now quite popular, especially with the banks and building societies, and it is leased by British Telecom under the commercial name "Kilostream". Because the access is directly into the digital transmission part of the network, it is not possible, while part of the network still retains analogue switching equipment, to offer Kilostream as a switched network service. Nevertheless, it provides a useful and readily available back-bone transmission facility on a leased line basis for a variety of private wide-area data networks.

In fact, it is also possible, under certain circumstances, to lease a complete 30 channel "group" transmission facility as a transparent 2.048 Mbits/s (usually referred to loosely as 2 Mbits/s) data transmission service. This service is offered under the commercial name of "Megastream". Although only available on certain high-traffic routes, it provides a useful back-bone for a number of nationwide private data networks with centralised computing and data processing facilities.

At the present time it is difficult to extend further the use of the PCM facilities for data transmission. However, progress made in recent times in digital electronics technology, together with the already widespread use of digital transmission for speech, has made it an attractive proposition to use digital switching techniques in place of the traditional electromechanical telephone switching systems. Telephone exchanges then become, in effect, special purpose digital computers which can be programmed, using Stored Program Control, to perform a range of sophisticated switching functions. Many telephone network operators are now gradually moving over to digital switching and, as this becomes widespread, it will be possible to use these facilities for data transmission on a switched service basis. We shall look at this development in some detail in the final chapter of this book.

MULTIPLEXORS AND CONCENTRATORS

We have seen that 64 kbits/s is now widely available, and 2 Mbits/s is not uncommon, for long-distance data transmission purposes. To make efficient use of these long-distance transmission facilities it is often possible to combine together signals from a number of different terminals to form a single stream of data. This can then be sent over a single transmission channel, thus making much more efficient use of the available transmission capacity.

There are two ways in which this combined use of a single channel can be implemented. Firstly, it can be achieved by straightforward multiplexing, usually on a time-division basis. The multiplexing may be carried out by taking a bit from each terminal in turn, or a byte or character from each terminal in turn, or indeed any appropriate size of packet to suit the application. The total bit-rate from all the user terminals cannot exceed the channel bit-rate, although terminals can be connected up to this rate. Thus up to 26 2.4 kbits/s terminals can be multiplexed onto a 64 kbits/s channel, leaving some bits available for framing purposes. It is not necessary that all the users operate at the same bit-rate, provided the total capacity is not exceeded. Thus a 64 kbits/s channel could service, say, three 9.6 kbits/s, four 4.8 kbits/s and six 2.4 kbits/s terminals, as shown in Fig.5.4. It is obviously simpler to arrange the multiplex frame structure if there is a simple arithmetical relationship between the contributing terminal bit-rates. At the far end of the

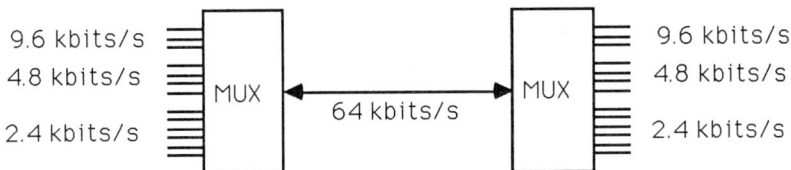

Fig.5.4 - Multiplexors with assorted input rates.

communication channel the contributing data streams are separated back into separate circuits for connection to the appropriate data terminal equipment.

In many applications the contributing channels are not always fully occupied. Under these circumstances it is possible, by suitably addressing the multiplex packets, to connect more terminals than simple multiplexing would normally allow. Use can thus be made of the statistical nature of the data sources to make even more efficient use of the communication channel. The multiplexing equipment, known as a statistical multiplexor (STATMUX) is more complex than the conventional multiplexor (MUX) and hence more expensive. However, on long-distance data links it is often possible to recoup the extra equipment cost by the saving in cost achieved by more efficient use of the transmission facility.

Often the data network consists of a number of remote terminals connected to a central computer. It may thus be unnecessary to separate the multiplexed data into separate channels at the point of receipt.

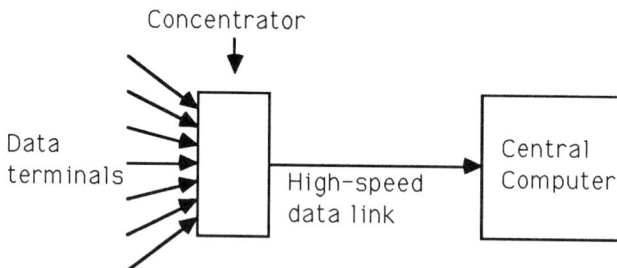

Fig.5.5 - Concentrator arrangement.

Instead, the data can be concentrated at a local point before transmission to the central data processor. Thus instead of providing a multiplexor, a concentrator can be used. The concentrator may simply assemble the data in packets in a way analogous to that used in the multiplexor, or it may be itself a miniprocessor that can carry out some preliminary data processing before the data is passed on to the remote mainframe computer. A typical concentrator arrangement is given in Fig.5.5.

A complex network arrangement may contain a mixture of multiplexors and concentrators, together eith a variety of transmission channels and modems. A typical complex wide area network configuration is given in Fig.5.6. There is an almost infinite variety of ways in which such a network might be configured, each being dependent on the user requirements and the available facilities.

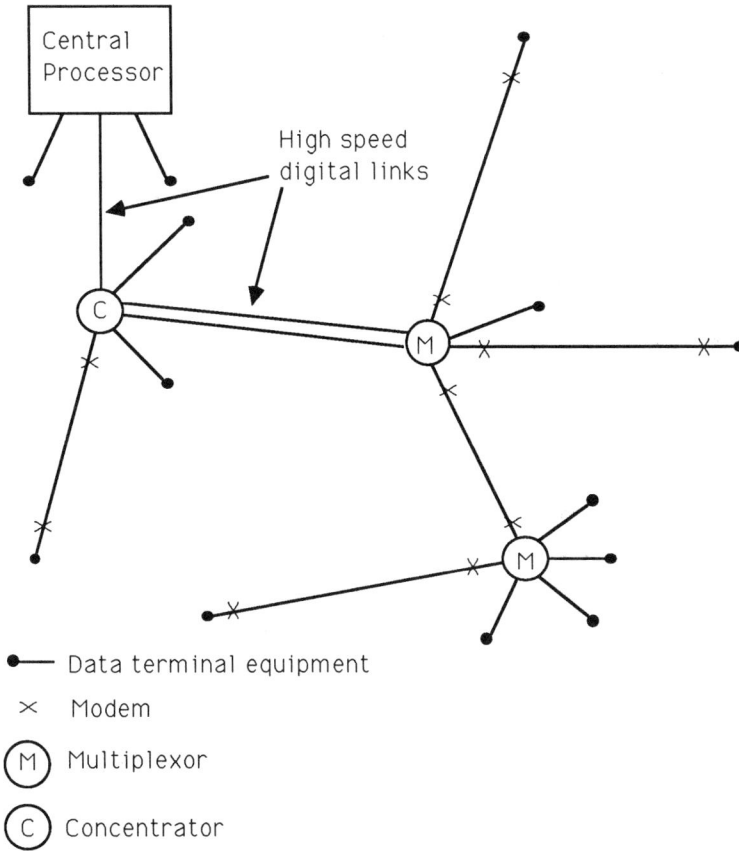

Fig.5.6 - Typical complex wide-area network.

PACKET-SWITCHED NETWORKS

Although the ISDN looks set to provide much of the data transmission requirements for the 21st century, it is likely that the majority of the traffic carried will still be basic telephony. Telephony places considerable restrictions on network design because transmission delays of any length of time cannot be tolerated and because successive data packets relating to the same signal must be received in strict sequence, otherwise speech intelligibility will be lost. This can lead to considerable inefficiency in the use of the network when much of the traffic consists of data transmission. Data is much more efficiently conveyed using the concept of store-and-forward network operation, which is based on the principle of packet-switching. A number of regional and national packet-switched networks have been provided specifically for data transmission applications. The operation of these networks most closely fits the OSI model. We shall therefore now take a look at packet-switching in closer detail.

Packet switched networks

PRINCIPLES OF PACKET SWITCHING

The telephone network is basically a circuit-switched network where a circuit is allocated for the whole duration of a call. The proportion of time during which information is actually being transmitted over the circuit if often quite small and thus far from efficient use is made of the network facilities. More efficient use of the network can be obtained if the network circuits are used to interconnect network nodes and information is passed from one node to another in a store-and-forward mode of operation. The message data is divided up into suitably dimensioned data packets, which enter the network through one of the nodes. They are then passed from node to node until they reach the node which serves the destination terminal. Packets forming part of the same message do not necessarily take the same route through the network or utilise the same circuits, as is illustrated in Fig.6.1.

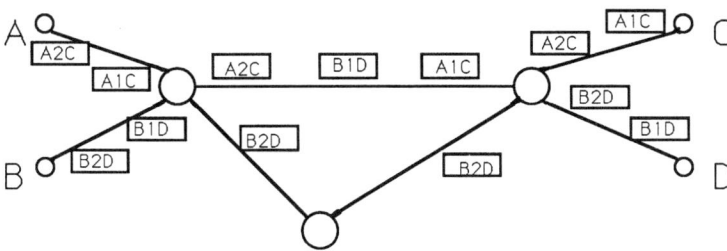

Fig. 6.1 Packet Switching.

However, as far as the sending and receiving terminals are concerned, a 'virtual circuit' is established between them so that they are generally unaware that the network is anything but circuit-switched. The network nodes are thus connected together by a logical channel rather than a direct circuit path. The choice of path through the network for each packet is determined by the traffic on the network at the time the packet enters the network. Because the traffic will be constantly changing, packets which form part of the same message may be routed through different nodes and circuits and may experience different delays in the store-and-forward procedure. In normal operation, therefore, it is possible for packets forming part of the same message to arrive at the receiving node in a different sequence to that in which they were entered at the sending node. It is therefore necessary for packets to be identified with a sequence number so that the receiving node is aware that the packets have been received out of sequence. In applications where the correct sequence is important, all packets have to be delayed at the receive node long enough for the packets to be resequenced before being passed on to the receive terminal. Alternatively, once a virtual call has been established, the same logical circuit can be used for all packets associated with the same message. Where the packet sequence is unimportant, the packets can be regarded as independent entities, usually referred to as 'datagrams'. In datagram operation each packet has to contain both source and destination addresses since, being an independent entity, it cannot make use of the information contained in the packets associated with setting-up the virtual call. Thus, although datagram operation makes more efficient use of the network transmission facilities, it requires a larger packet overhead than would be required if all the packets associated with a single message follow the same route once the virtual circuit has been established.

HDLC AND X25

The OSI model layer 3 protocol generally used with packet-switched networks is that defined in CCITT recommendation X25. X25 operates within a layer 2 protocol known as Link Access Protocol - Balanced (LAP-B). LAP-B is the asynchronous balanced mode (ABM) version of the more general layer 2 protocol known as High-level Data Link Control (HDLC). The ABM version of HDLC is used for point-to-point transmission where both nodes or stations have equal status. Either can therefore take on the role of primary, the other then becoming the secondary station. The alternative version of HDLC, the normal response mode (NRM), is used in multidrop situations, where the master station always takes on the role of primary and the other stations on the multidrop are always regarded as secondaries. The basic frame structure is common to both the NRM and ABM versions of HDLC and is therefore directly applicable to LAP-B. The HDLC (LAP-B) frame format is shown in Fig.6.2.

Flag	Add.	Cont.	Information field (X25)	Frame check sequence	Flag
8 bits	8 bits	8 bits	Variable	16 bits	8 bits

Fig.6.2 - HDLC frame structure.

LAP-B in turn utilises the physical interface specified in CCITT recommendations X21 or X21 bis. X21 bis is compatible with CCITT recommendation V24 for a data terminal interface with modems operating over the public telephone network. It should perhaps be emphasised here that V24 defines the data terminal equipment interface to the modem and is not concerned with the interface between the modem and the line itself. The modems themselves therefore form part of the conceptual physical connection. The V24 interface is thus independent of both modulation technique and data throughput rate.

The X21 data stream is divided into frames which are delimited by a flag sequence consisting of eight bits. The flag octet used in HDLC consists of the bit pattern 01111110. To prevent false flag indications occurring due to the occurrence of the flag octet pattern in the rest of the frame field, a technique known as 'bit stuffing' is used. Whenever five consecutive 1s occur in the data, an extra 0 is inserted (stuffed) into the digit stream following the fifth 1 digit, whatever the next digit is. Thus the sequence of six 1 digits is unique to the flag. Because a 0 is stuffed whether the next digit is a 0 or 1, on receipt of five consecutive 1s it is a simple matter to remove the next 0 from the digit sequence, thus reverting to the original binary data packet content. Because the size of the HDLC frame is in any case variable, the packet format is not impaired by the insertion of occasional extra 0 digits. The bit stuffing is performed on the complete packet format and the basic packet structure is performed before the bit stuffing operation is carried out.

The HDLC packet proper comprises four fields. The first field consists of 8 bits known as the Address field. The address specified in this field is that of the secondary node, that is, the node corresponding to the called party. The node associated with the calling party always acts as the primary node. Thus all communication processes originate from the primary. Messages originating from the primary therefore contain the address of the node to which the message is directed. Response messages, however, contain the address of the node from which the response originates. Because of the network strategy, the other address is implicit in the interchange procedure and the single address field is sufficient for network housekeeping purposes.

The second field consists of a further 8 bits and is referred to as the Control field. The significance of the bits depends on the packet type and certain of the bits are actually used to define the type of packet. The significance of the bits for each packet type is given in Fig.6.3.

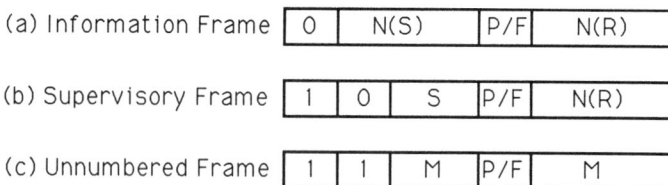

(a) Information Frame

0	N(S)	P/F	N(R)

(b) Supervisory Frame

1	0	S	P/F	N(R)

(c) Unnumbered Frame

1	1	M	P/F	M

Fig.6.3 - HDLC control field structure.

If the first bit is a 0, then the packet is an information frame, that is, it is the normal type of frame used when there is information to be transmitted. In this case, bits 2 to 4 and 6 to 8 are sequence check numbers N(S) and N(R). Packet switching does not rely on semi-permanent circuits being established for the whole duration of the call. Instead, packets are routed individually through the network by any suitably available link. Since consecutive packets may take different routes, with different delay factors, it is possible for packets to arrive at the receiving node in a different sequence to that in which they were transmitted. To ensure the receiver is aware of this, each succeeding packet is numbered consecutively in binary notation modulo-8 in the three digit slots designated N(S). Since differential delays in excess of eight packet periods are highly unlikely, the use of modulo-8 counting is generally adequate for all practical purposes. The sequence numbering in the N(S) sub-field is carried out independently by both the primary and the secondary. The N(R) sub-field is used to indicate the number of the next packet in sequence that the node expects to receive and therefore acts as an acknowledgement to the sender that the previous packet has been correctly received. The sender can thus keep tabs on which of his message packets have been received and decide whether action is necessary to retransmit any packets received in error or not received at all.

If the first bit of the Control field is 1, then the second bit also defines the packet type. If the second bit is a 0, then the frame is a supervisory frame. The supervisory frame is used to send the N(R) acknowledgement when there is no information to be sent on which the acknowledgement can be sent 'piggy-back'. As there is no information to be sent, there is no sequence number N(S) to be sent. The other two bits, shown as S in Fig.6.3(b), can then be used to signal the state of the receiving terminal. The two bits can be used to signal four states. These are:

(a) Receive Ready: Indicates that the node has correctly received a packet and that it is ready to receive the next packet in sequence, which it expects to be number N(R).

(b) Receive Not Ready: Indicates that the node has correctly received a packet and that the next packet it expects to receive is number N(R). However, it also indicates that the terminal is temporarily not ready to receive it.

(c) Reject: Indicates that a packet has been received in error. N(R) will therefore indicate the number of the packet from which retransmission should commence.

(d) Selective Reject: Indicates a specific packet has been received in error and requests retransmission of that packet only. This can only be used with sophisticated networks which have resequencing facilities available.

If both the first and second bits in the control field are 1, then the frame is an 'unnumbered frame'.   Unnumbered frames are normally used to communicate commands and responses for the purposes of link housekeeping rather than for the interchange of information between network nodes.   As they are not normally associated with the transmission of information packets, there is no requirement for packet sequence numbers.   Bits 3,4,6,7 and 8, designated M in Fig.6.3(c), are thus all available for command and response signals.   Thus 32 different signalling combinations can be specified using the M field.   The list is complex and only of specialised interest.   The reader is directed to the CCITT recommendation X25 or one of the specialised books on packet networks if further details are required.

Whatever the type of Control field, the fifth bit is always what is known as the Poll/Final bit, designated P/F in Figs.6.3 (a), (b) and (c). In frames orignated by the primary the P/F bit is set to 1 to poll the secondary, that is, to instruct the secondary to issue a response.   In frames originated by the secondary the P/F bit is set to 1 to indicate to the primary that it is sending the final frame in a message sequence.

The HDLC Information field carries the X25 data packet which is itself structured to control the level 3 network functions.   We will defer further discussion of the X25 format until we have completed our discussion of HDLC.

The final field in the HDLC frame is the frame check sequence.   This consists of 16 bits obtained using a cyclic redundancy check code over the Address, Control and Information fields of the HDLC frame.   The characteristic polynomial used in HDLC is the CCITT V41 polynomial

$$X^{16} + X^{12} + X^5 + 1$$

as described earlier in Chapter 4.   The frame check sequence is generated before bit stuffing is carried out.

The X25 level 3 packet occupies the Information field in the HDLC level 2 frame. The higher order of the control exercised at level 3 means that the X25 packet structure is more complex than that of HDLC and there is a much wider range of packet types.   Space does not permit a full discussion of each type of X25 packet. We shall therefore have to content ourselves with a look at the general packet structure so that we can at least appreciate the general philosophy of X25 operation.

A generalised format structure for X25 packets is given in Fig.6.4. The packet firstly contains a Format Identifier which defines the format of the rest of the packet field. This is always followed by a Logical Channel Identifier which carries the number of the logical channel. Each call is allocated a logical number so that packets related to the same call can be identified. This is followed by a Packet Type field which specifies the function of the packet.

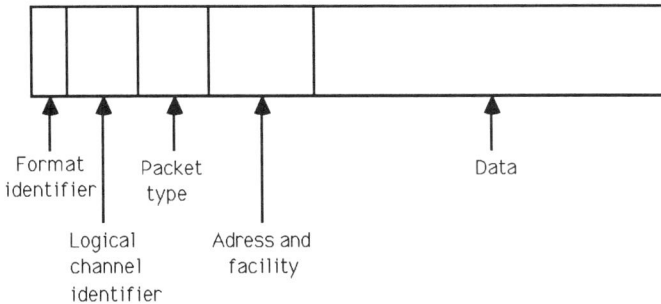

Fig.6.4 - Generalised X25 format structure.

Packets can be of several types. Packets involved in call initiation will contain full address information in the next field slot. Subsequent packets do not require full address information since the packet routing is now under the control of the Logical Channel Identifier. The address/facility field can then be utilised for sequence numbering or acknowledgement information. Acknowledgement and Control packets do not require a data field. Information packets will contain a data field of variable length, usually with a maximum size of 128 octets.

THE PROVISION OF PACKET-SWITCHED NETWORKS

Packet-switched networks, both for public and private use, exist in most European countries, throughout North America and in many other parts of the world. These are mostly accessed through X25 interfaces. In the UK, an X25 packet-switched network is provided by British Telecom and is accessible to users at least in most of the larger towns and cities. In some cases the access has to be via the public telephone network using Datel modems with a V24 interface. Many of the world's packet-switched networks can be interconnected to provide international data communication at X25 level.

There is sometimes a requirement to connect data terminal equipment to the packet-switched network which does not contain sufficient intelligence to operate through an X25 interface. Such terminals normally operate in an asynchronous character mode, providing an interface through a serial character stream. Another possible requirement is the interconnection of local area networks through the public packet-switched network. To perform these functions a Packet Assembler/Disassembler (PAD) is required. The PAD converts the character stream into X25 packets for transmission through the packet-switched network and also converts the X25 packets back into asynchronous character format before passing on to the receiving terminal equipment. Three separate X series CCITT recommendations are associated with the PAD, namely X3, X28 and X29. We shall not go into details of these recommendations here. Suffice it to say that because of the three separate recommendations relating to the PAD, the standard is often referred to as the 'Triple X' standard. Because PADs may be required for a variety of different terminals and applications, there are several options within the Triple X recommendations and a range of PADs are available for specific applications. More complex general-purpose PADs can also be obtained which can be programmed for several different applications.

Local area networks.

INTRODUCTION.

A variety of Local Area Network achitectures have been proposed from time to time to meet the needs of various users. These are normally classified according to the network topology as shown in Fig.7.1.

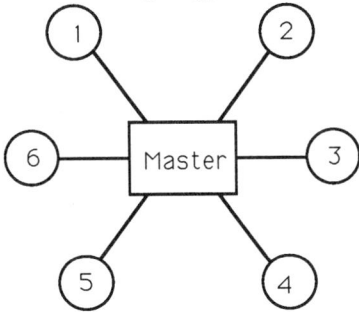

(a) star network

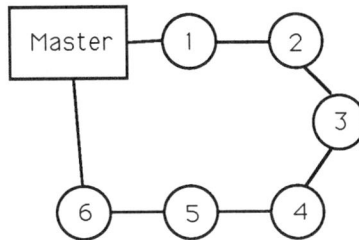

(b) loop network

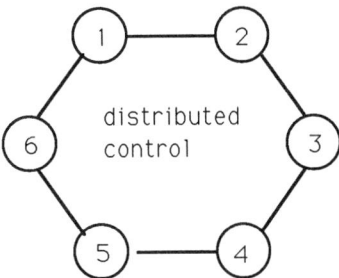

(c) ring network

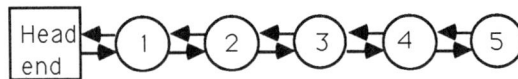

i) repeatered

or

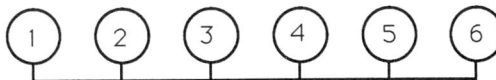

ii) common highway

(d) bus architecture

Fig.7.1 - Local area network configurations.

A star network is based on a central hub which effects the network control. The terminals are normally connected by separate circuits to the hub, although multiplexing may sometimes be used to provide multiple circuits on a single physical pair. An example of a star network is one based upon the PABX (Private automatic branch exchange). Star networks are normally circuit-switched and provide transparent half or full-duplex transmission. Because of the circuit transparency, the network is unable to carry out code, speed or protocol conversion. They can, however, generally be used for carrying voice traffic as well as digital communication.

In a loop system, the devices are connected to a common highway which takes the form of a closed loop. One station normally acts as master and polls the other stations in turn, requesting them to transmit if they have any data to send. The loop network has two basic disadvantages. Firstly, the polling strategy means that the response time is relatively slow compared to other configurations. Secondly, the basic master/slave relationship places unnecessary restrictions on network operation.

The most commonly used configurations are the ring and bus architectures and we shall consider these in more detail in the rest of this chapter.

RINGS

In the ring architecture, the devices are again connected in a 'loop' but all the devices now participate in the control strategy. In principle the interconnection of the devices may be either common highway or by interconnection of adjacent devices, the devices themselves forming part of the transmission ring. In practice the latter method is usually preferred. In this method the data signal is detected at each node point and then retransmitted to the next node point around the ring. The network is thus referred to as an 'active' network, as opposed to the 'passive' network where the data signal passes directly from the sender to the receiver without further amplification or regeneration. Several strategies exist for inserting new data into the highway. One method is 'register insertion', where data on the highway is temporarily buffered and new data is inserted ahead of it. This strategy is illustrated in Fig.7.2.

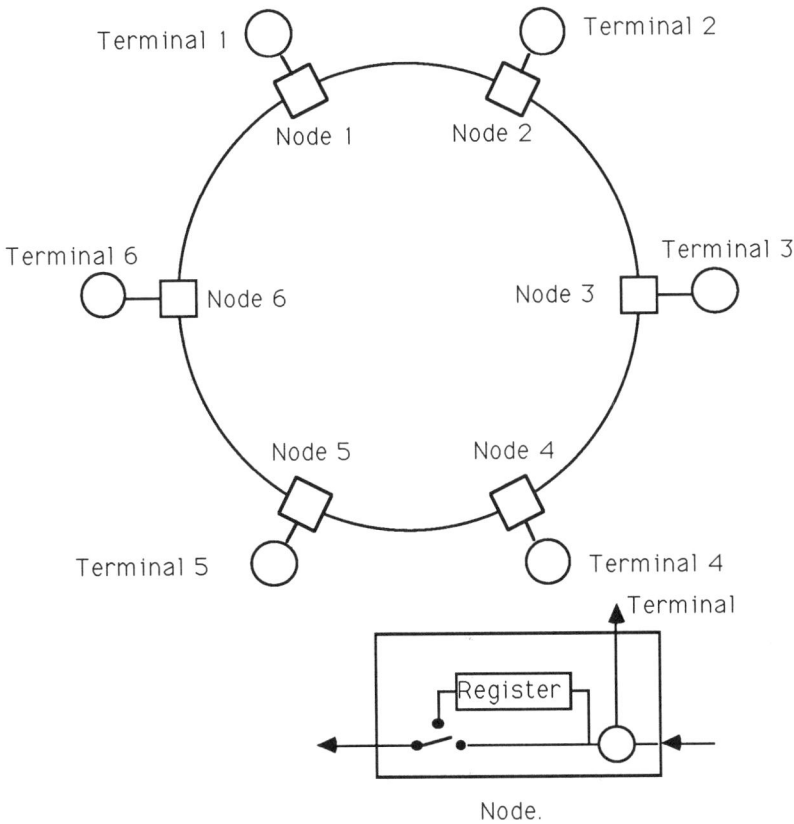

Fig.7.2 - Register insertion network access.

When there is no data to be transmitted, each node is connected directly to the next node and a unique pattern of digits, referred to as the 'token', is circulated around the ring.   When a terminal has data to transmit, the data is loaded into the register at the node and the token is awaited.   As soon as the token has passed the node, the switch it changed so that the register at that node is connected into the ring The data is then circulated behind the token to each of the subsequent nodes in turn. If any of these nodes wish to send data, they then load it into their register and again await the token.   As soon as the token has passed the node, the switch is changed so that a further register is inserted in the network.   The newly added data thus circulates behind the token but ahead of any other data already circulating in the network.   As the data passes through each node in turn, the node examines the address field to see whether the data is intended for that node.   If so, the data is read and any appropriate acknowledgement is added. The data is, however, then passed on until it reaches the register of the terminal responsible for its insertion. At this point, the register is switched out of circuit so that the acknowledgement can be checked and the register reloaded with the next batch of data for transmission, as it becomes available. The node then again awaits the token before reinserting the register with the new batch of data. Register insertion was used on some early ring configured LANs but has subsequently declined in popularity in favour of the alternative 'token-passing' and 'empty slot' strategies.

The token-passing strategy is an alternative to register-insertion where new data is inserted after, instead of before, the current data and where the token follows the data circulating in the ring. When a node with data ready to transmit detects the token, it temporarily removes the token, adds its own new data, and then again appends the token at the end of the transmission. The strategy is thus similar in principle to register-insertion but any new data now follows, rather than preceeds, the current data circulating in the network. There are a number of commercially available ring-based networks which operate using the token-passing strategy.

A further strategy is the method known as 'empty slot', in which the highway is effectively time assigned into separate slots and a terminal waits until it detects an empty slot before transmitting. Probably the best-known ring topology employing the empty slot control strategy is the 'Cambridge Ring'. We shall now look at the Cambridge Ring in a little more detail.

THE CAMBRIDGE RING

The Cambridge Ring employs the empty slot strategy. Data is transmitted around the ring at base-band, that is, the signals are not modulated onto a carrier as, we shall later see, is the case with broad-band systems. A line code is used, however, to ensure transitions occur in the data sequence so that bit-timing can be recovered by the recipient. The line code used with the Cambridge Ring is the Wal 1 or Manchester Code, described earlier in Chapter 3. The bit transmission rate is 10 Mbits/s. The slot frame consists of 38 bits. There must be sufficient transmission delay around the ring for it to contain at least one whole frame and a couple of extra bits to separate the first and last bits around the ring. There can, of course, be a multiple of frames, each separated by a least two bits from each other. In practice Cambridge Rings almost always operate with only a single slot circulating, requiring a minimum of 40 bit locations around the ring. Bits are observed by a station one at a time, being held at the station for a 1-bit period. There is thus a single-bit delay associated with each station. If the connections between stations are fairly long, there is a possibility of further bits being stored owing to transmission delays, but this is not common. Any additional delay required to achieve the minimum of 40 bits stored is provided by the insertion of a shift register in the ring, usually at the monitor station. The monitor station is not a network terminal. It is provided to monitor the network operation and to restore the slot pattern should this be disturbed by transmission errors or faulty terminals. A layout of a Cambridge Ring, showing the delays, is given in Fig.7.3(a). The slot bit pattern is shown in Fig.7.3(b). Pattern synchronism is established when the network is first switched on. Each receiver thus knows when to expect the start bit. The start bit is always binary 1 and the surplus bits are always binary 0. It is thus a simple matter to check each time whether synchronism has been affected by bit deletion or insertion, providing this is contained within reasonable limits. The second bit in the frame indicates whether the slot is empty or full acccording to whether it contains a 0 or a 1 respectively. On receipt of an empty indication, a station may seize the slot if it has data to transmit by substituting a 1 for the 0 in the Full/Empty location and filling the rest of the frame as appropriate. On receipt of a full indication one of three actions can be taken. Firstly, if the station knows that it filled the slot on the previous pass, it will substitute 0 for 1 in the Full/Empty and adjacent Monitor bit locations and check the response bits to see whether further action is necessary. It then passes on the slot marked as empty, signifying that the rest of the bits left in the slot are no longer valid and may be overwritten. If the station was not responsible for filling the slot, it will check the destination address to find out whether the packet is intended for it. If so, it will read the source address and the data bits and update the response bits as appropriate. If the destination address is that of another station, it just passes the bits on without further action.

The third bit in the frame is the Monitor bit and is used by the Monitor Station to check that packets are not circulating continuously around the ring thus preventing

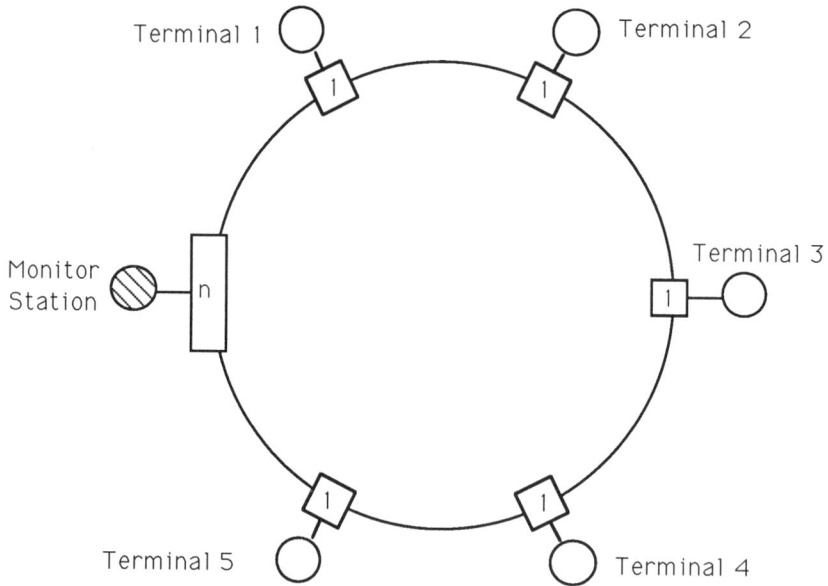

(a) Ring layout
(showing bit delays)

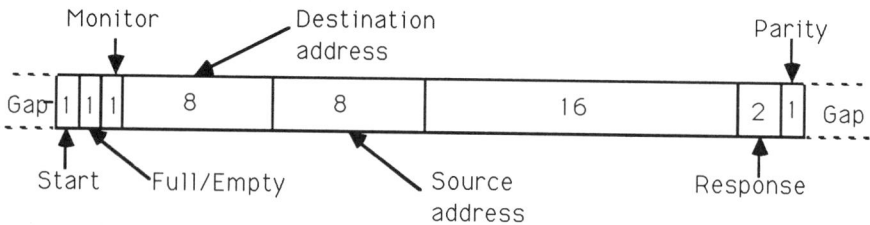

(b) Slot bit pattern

Fig.7.3 - Details of Cambridge ring.

other users from seizing the slot. Whenever a 'full' slot passes the monitor station, the monitor bit is checked to see whether it contains a 0 or 1. If it contains a 0, then the monitor station replaces it with a 1. This 1 will then be reset to 0 when the slot is marked as empty on return to its originator. If, therefore, the monitor station receives a 'full' slot with the monitor bit also set to 1, this indicates that, for some reason, the slot has not been marked as empty by its originator. The full slot is therefore rotating around the ring and preventing further seizure of the slot by another user.   The monitor station has therefore to take action to re-initialise the slot pattern and to record a network failure.

The next group of eight bits (byte) contains the destination address of any information in the data field and is filled by the station seizing the slot for message transmission.   It is deleted by overwriting when a new message is written into the field.

The next byte contains the source address of any information in the data field and is filled and deleted in similar fashion to the destination address.

The next two bytes contain 16 data bits which constitute a packet of the text of the message to be transmitted.   They are, again, filled and deleted in a manner similar to the destination address.   Because each packet only contains 16 bits, messages usually consist of several packets sent sequentially as empty slots become available.

The next two bits are the response bits, which are used to acknowledge the receipt of packets by the recipient.   Both bits are normally set to zero by the sender when a slot is seized.   The recipient then changes the pair of bits into one of the three remaining bit patterns to indicate that the packet has been accepted, or that it has been rejected because the receive terminal is busy processing data previously received, or that it has been rejected because the transmitter has not been selected. The last response is used by a receive terminal that is awaiting further packets of data from another terminal which together form a single complete message.   This is necessary because a single data slot is normally insufficient to hold a complete message sequence.   When the transmitter receives the response bits, it will then know whether the packet has been received or whether it has to retransmit a rejected packet.   If the response bits have not been altered by the recipient, the transmitter will deduce that there is no active node on the network with this address.

The final bit in the frame is a parity bit.   The parity of the packet is checked at each node and failure in the parity check is noted.   Repeated failure of parity may be taken as an indication of a failure of the preceding node.   Various actions can be taken on detection of parity failures depending on the network user requirements. If the monitor station has diagnostic capabilities, it is usual to pass the appropriate information on to it to initiate further action.

DATA THROUGHPUT AND ACCESS TIME

The empty slot protocol is essentially a 'fair share' protocol. Since the empty slot must be passed on each time it is used, every other user has an opportunity to send a packet before the initial user can send a second packet. Assuming a bit-rate on the ring of 10 Mbits/s and 16 data bits in each packet of 40 bits overall size, a solitary user on the ring could use every other packet and thus obtain a data throughput rate of 2 Mbits/s. The longest wait for access (the receipt of the first full/empty bit) would be 4 μs. However, with 250 users on the network simultaneously, the data throughput per user would drop to 8 kbits/s and the maximum access time would increase to 1 ms. Thus the effect on a user of increasing traffic on the network is a progressive reduction in data throughput rate, although access would be guarranteed within the time equivalent to the time required to transmit a single packet containing 16 data bits at the data throughput rate applicable at the time.

BRAIDED AND SELF-HEALING RINGS

A major disadvantage of the active ring is that a failure of a single node is catastrophic in that this leads directly to a complete loss of communication throughout the whole of the ring. Of course a failure in any link would be equally catastrophic, but the links are inherently more reliable than the nodes and are thus less likely to be the source of network failure. Network reliability can be improved by adding extra 'redundant' elements to the network. There are two basic strategies used with active ring networks; braided rings and duplicated rings.

In the braided ring, additional links are provided to interconnect nodes to the next-but-one nodes around the ring as well as to the adjacent nodes as shown in Fig.7.4.

Should any node fail it can be by-passed by means of the extra link across the node. The technique is useful for register-insertion and token-passing rings but, if used with slotted-rings, then steps must be taken to ensure that the slot bit-pattern is maintained. This can be achieved by incorporating additional delay elements in the braid by-pass to keep the ring delay constant in the presence of faults. The disadvantage of the braided ring is that up to three times the amount of cabling is required compared to the simple ring configuration.

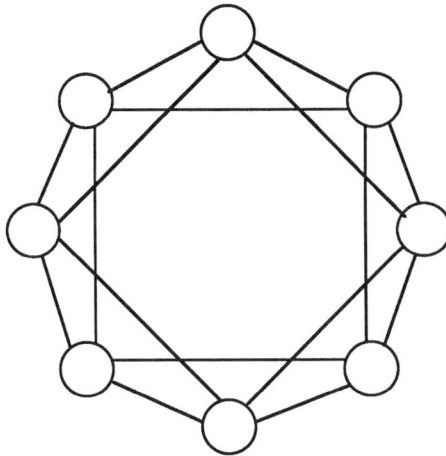

Fig.7.4 - Braided ring configuration.

In duplicated rings, both the nodes and the links are duplicated.   There are a variety of ways in which this can be implemented.   Firstly, the ring can simply be duplicated as shown in Fig.7.5

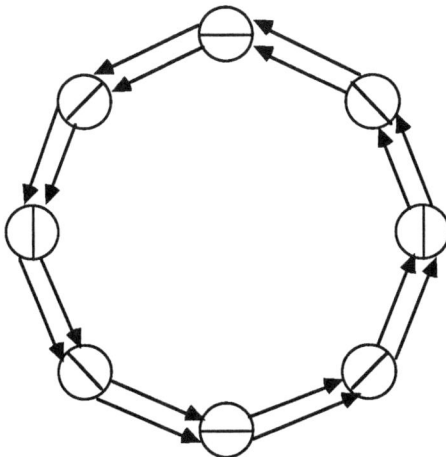

Fig.7.5 - Duplicated ring configuration.

The additional ring can be operated simply as a stand-by, being brought into operation on failure of the main ring. Alternatively, multiple faults can be tolerated by using sections of either the main ring or the stand-by as appropriate. To obtain more efficient operation, normally both rings can be used to carry data, the traffic being shared between the rings. In the event of a failure, the appropriate sections will be used, the traffic handling capability being reduced by 50%. Again, more than one fault can be tolerated, provided a complete circuit around the ring can be maintained by the use of sections from one or other of the ring configurations.

A further improvement in toleration of multiple faults, especially of failure of both main and stand-by units in a single node or link, can be achieved by operation of the rings in opposite directions as shown in Fig.7.6.

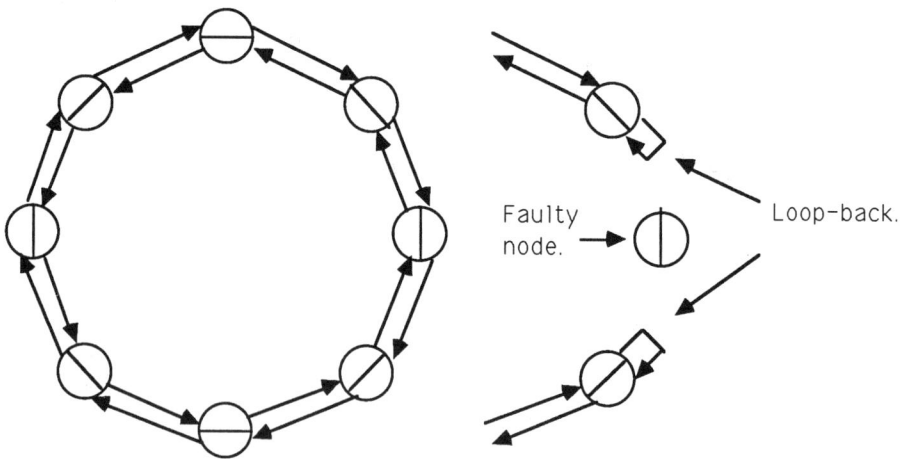

Fig.7.6 - Duplicated ring with self-healing capability.

Faulty nodes or links can now be isolated by loop-back techniques whilst maintaining full interconnection of the remaining nodes. Automatic techniques for detecting and isolating faulty nodes have been developed to produce 'self-healing' networks. Multiple failures may cause isolation of some functional nodes, but communication between sub-groups of nodes can still be maintained. Other configurations using asymmetrical duplication have been proposed which give even better protection against multiple failures.   However, these require complex control algorithms and thus have not so far been incorporated into any practical LAN implementations.

BUSES

The bus architecture implies an open-ended highway topology, as opposed to the closed arrangement of the loop and ring networks.   There are two basic bus strategies, the repeated bus and the common highway, as illustrated in Fig.7.1. The former is an active network in which the data signal is regenerated and retransmitted by each station in turn, as with the active ring.   In the common highway strategy, the network highway is passive in that the signal passes directly along the bus from sender to recipient without further amplification or regeneration.   We consider first the common highway passive bus network structure.

CSMA/CD

In passive bus networks, the terminals are connected directly onto the common highway.   To avoid simultaneous use of the highway by two or more senders, terminals wishing to transmit contend for the bus using a technique known as CSMA/CD (carrier-sense multiple-access with collision detection).   In this mode of operation, terminals wishing to transmit first 'listen' to the highway and then transmit only if they sense that there is no other signal already in existence on the bus.   If the terminal senses that the highway is already in use, it waits for a short period and then checks the highway again.   When it finds the highway free, it sends its data and awaits acknowledgement.   The wait period is necessary rather than a continuous monitoring of the bus as, if several terminals are waiting to send, on detecting the end of transmission all the waiting terminals would commence to send simultaneously, resulting in data collision.   Various techniques, involving random wait times and exponentially increasing waiting periods, have been proposed for avoiding recurrent collisions on heavily used highways.   Collisions are detected by highway monitoring to check whether the tranmitted data has been corrupted by simultaneous transmissions.

The best-known CSMA/CD bus network is that known as 'Ethernet', in fact Ethernet is so well-known that the title is becoming widely used to describe all CSMA/CD networks based on the passive bus architecture, even though it is strictly a commercial brand name for a specific group of manufacturers product (Digital Equipment Corporation, Intel Corporation and Xerox Corporation).

ETHERNET

Ethernet is a CSMA/CD bus network. The stations are connected to a common bus highway. The network is therefore passive; that is the signals pass directly from the sender to the receiver. They do not pass through any other stations or any other repeaters as they generally do in the ring strategies. Ethernet therefore contrasts with the Cambridge Ring described earlier in this chapter, which is an example of an active network. Transmission is at 10 Mbits/s and base-band transmission is used. Since the network is passive, the network is not intrinsically synchronous and it is therefore necessary to synchronise the sending and receiving terminals each time a transmission path is established. Each packet, therefore, has to commence with a synchronising preamble to ensure synchronism is achieved before the transmission of meaningful data commences. The preamble normally consists of a sequence of 32 bits. This is followed by the Destination and Source Address fields.

Sync	Destination address	Source address	Packet type	Data	Check-sum
32 bits	48 bits	48 bits	16 bits	Variable 45-1500 bytes	32 bits

Fig.7.7 - Ethernet frame field allocation.

Because of the possibility of interworking of local Ethernets and to allow portability of terminals between separate Ethernets, it is considered to be desirable that terminal addresses should be universally unique, rather than unique only within the confines of the local network. Each of the address fields therefore consists of 48 bits, which gives a possibility of over 280 billion (2.8×10^{14}) different addresses.

The next 16 bits are used to define the packet type. Then follows the data field, which can vary to anything between 45 and 1500 bytes, depending on the individual message requirement. A minimum packet size is necessary to ensure satisfactory operation of the contention procedure. For messages requiring less than 45 bytes, the data field must be filled with dummy data up to the minimum size. The maximum field size is necessary to prevent a single user monopolising the transmission facility. On Ethernet, therefore, a complete message usually occupies only one packet, whereas in the Cambridge Ring it is unusual, except for acknowledgement messages, for a message to be contained within a single packet.

The data field is followed by a Check-sum field of 32 bits produced using a Cyclic Redundancy Check-sum Code over the address and data fields. The basic Ethernet frame is shown in Fig.7.7.

A station wishing to transmit monitors the bus to see whether transmission by another station is already in progress. If so, the station withdraws and waits for a short, randomly determined period of time before contending for the highway again. The random delay prevents several waiting stations attempting to acquire the bus simultaneously when transmission ceases. If the bus is clear, the station begins transmitting its synchronising pattern. However, it continues to monitor the bus for a further period equivalent to the longest transmission delay likely to be encountered on the bus. In this way the station can detect any collisions that might occur owing to two (or more) stations detecting the same silence and both commencing to transmit before receiving data already sent by the other terminal but delayed in propagation along the bus.

The maximum length for a single Ethernet bus is about 500 metres. For lengths greater than this, repeaters are required. Up to a 100 tap tranceivers can be connected on to one Ethernet segment. The tranceiver connects the user station interface cable to the common bus highway. Larger systems consist of several segments interconnected via repeaters. The repeaters act as an interchange between the two interconnected segments. Such an arangement is illustrated in Fig.7.8.

PERFORMANCE OF CSMA/CD BUS NETWORKS

The contention feature of CSMA/CD bus networks means that under heavy load the

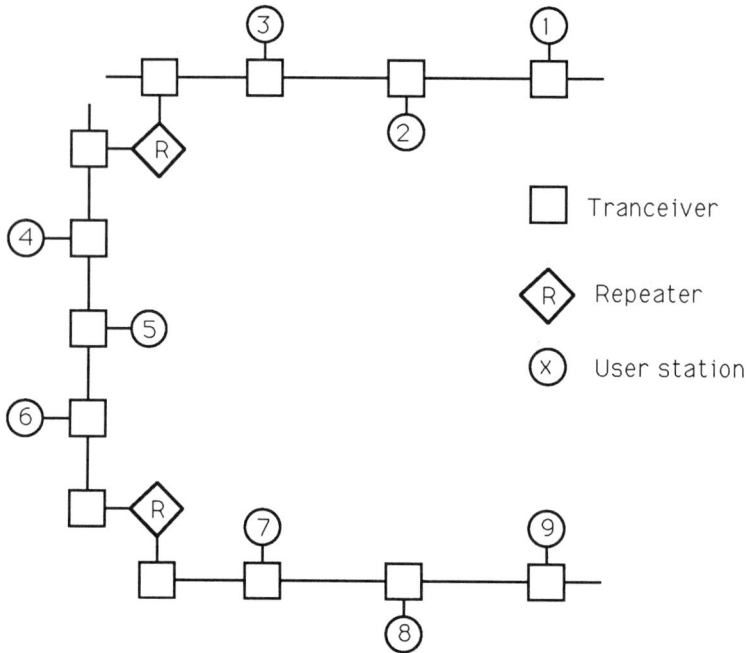

Fig.7.8 - Multi-segment Ethernet configuration.

network does not operate on the 'fair-share' basis that is characteristic of the Cambridge and token-passing rings. Instead, access is based on the statistical laws of chance. It is possible, under heavy traffic conditions, for a user to make repeated abortive attempts at access, whereas another user may be lucky enough to access the network at the first attempt. There is, therefore, the risk of unpredictable lengthy delays in obtaining access to the network. However, once access has been obtained, the user gets exclusive use of the network for the transmission of the whole message, except for very long messages in excess of 1500 bytes, giving a data throughput rate of 10 Mbits/s. The performance characteristics as seen by the user, therefore, are just the reverse of those displayed by the Cambridge Ring. Whereas increasing traffic on the ring means a progressive slowing down of the data throughput but with immediate access to the network guarranteed, with the CSMA/CD bus the data throughput is maintained at the bus transmission rate but access to the network can involve a considerable and unpredictable wait before the bus is acquired.

BROADBAND NETWORKS

Active bus configured networks are used where longer distances or higher transmission rates, or both, are required than can be obtained with passive bus networks. These networks ususally employ what is known as broadband transmission, as opposed to baseband transmission. In broadband transmission the data is modulated onto a carrier in a manner similar to that described in chapter 2. The better performance is therefore obtained at a cost of more complex line-driving equipment. One advantage of broadband, however, is that, by the use of multiple carrier frequencies, it is possible to use frequency multiplex techniques to obtain multiple logical channels over a single transmission path.

In an active bus network, two logical paths are provided between the nodes, transmitting in opposite directions along the bus. The two paths are linked at one end of the bus through a device known as the 'head-end'. Stations initiate data transmssion on the path towards the head-end and receive on the path from the headend. Data arriving at a node which is neither the originator or recipient of the message is simply repeated and passed on the the next node in the appropriate direction of transmission. All transmissions will pass through the head-end. The head-end can therefore act as the network monitor.

Similarities between the active bus and the active ring suggest that token-passing would be an appropriate access protocol for use with the active bus. Many networks do in fact make use of token-passing, although some make use of a modified form of CSMA/CD. To obtain the features of CMSA/CD on an active network involves rather more complex control strategies than are generally necessary for a passive bus. However, the enhanced performance obtained using broadband techniques can largely offset the cost of the increased access complexity.

The two directions of transmission between nodes can be achieved simply by using two separate transmission paths. However, using broadband transmission, it is an easy matter to obtain full-duplex operation using frequency-division-mutliplex techniques. This involves using different carrier frequencies for the send and receive channels so that the two signals occupy two different frequency bands within the single transmission medium. Where two separate transmission paths are used, the head-end simply consists of a repeater which transfers the data stream from the transmit to the receive path.   In the case of broadband systems using frequency-division-multiplex to obtain the two channels, the head-end will consist of a frequency translator which changes the data carrier frequency from that of the transmit channel to that of the receive channel.

In fact it is possible to divide the total transmission bandwidth into several transmission bands so that the network is effectively a multi-bus network.   This possibility can be used in a number of ways.   Firstly, using a CSMA/CD strategy, it is possible for users to contend on more than one of the multi-buses, thus reducing the possibility of unfortunate long delays in access.   Also, with both token-passing and CSMA/CD protocols, it is possible to give priority to certain users by restricting access to one or more of the multibuses to high-priority users only. Modems which may be switched to change carrier frequency so as to allow access onto more than one of the multi-buses are known as 'frequency-agile modems'.

Since modulation is used on broadband systems, it is possible to combine digital and analogue transmission over the same circuit.   Thus a coaxial cable network may be used to carry a digital service at data rates of up to several Mbits/s in combination with a multichannel video service conveying television-quality pictures.

OPTICAL FIBRE LANS

Optical fibres have recently found widespread application as a transmission medium for telecommunications networks.   Signals are conveyed as a light beam along a glass or transparent plastic fibre.   Glass fibres are dimensionally very much smaller and offer a considerably greater transmission bandwidth than the conventional metal conductor.   Using a fibre the thickness of a human hair, it is possible to convey data at several gigabits per second. (1 Gbit/s = 10^9 bits/s or 1000 Mbits/s.) The light beam may be modulated using either analogue or digital techniques, although non-linearities in the transducers make digital modulation the preferred method.   Besides large transmission capability and small size, other advantages of optical fibres are high immunity to interference, electrically non-conducting and therefore non-hazardous in explosive and combustible environments and high security against unauthorised interception.   These features make optical fibres an attractive proposition for local area networks.

Fibre networks are intrinsically broad-band networks. One disadvantage of optical fibres is the difficulty of tapping into the light path. They are not therefore suitable for passive bus operation.

The earliest standard for optical fibre LANs is the Fibre-optic Distributed Data Interface (FDDI). This uses a dual optical fibre ring, one for each direction of transmission around the ring. Light-emitting diodes (LEDs) are used to produce the modulated optical signal at an effective transmission rate of 100 Mbits/s. The network operates using a token-passing protocol with information flowing in either direction around the ring. One direction can be considered as the primary signal path, the other direction being used as a back-up in case of failure of the primary. Alternatively, full use of both directions can be made, effectively doubling the transmission capability, providing it is acceptable to operate at the nominal 100 Mbits/s rate under fault conditions. Loop-back on failure of a node, or node by-pass, can be used to obtain fault-tolerant operation.

A form of CSMA/CD using optical fibres can be implemented by means of a star-configured fibre network. An optical splitter can be used at the star point to obtain multiple-access by contention to any other user on the network as shown in Fig.7.9. At the time of writing this form of operation is still under development, but it seems certain that we shall hear more of this technique in the near future.

Frequency-division-multiplex can be achieved on optical fibre by the use of

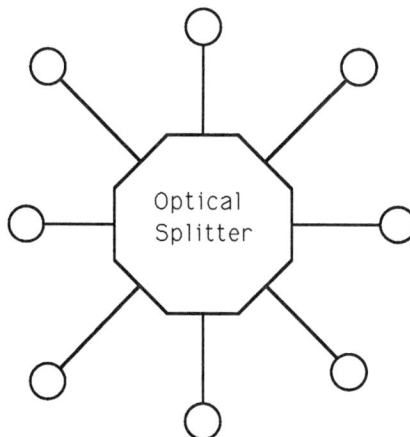

Fig.7.9 - Star network using optical splitter to obtain CSMA/CD.

different coloured light-source emissions. Since it is common practice to define light colour bands in terms of wavelength rather than frequency, the technique is usually referred to as wave-length division multiplexing (wdm), rather than fdm, when applied to optical transmission systems. Optical broad-band networks are already in use for combined analogue and digital signal transmission.

Very much higher transmission capabilities are possible using lasers instead of light-emitting diodes (LEDs) as optical signalling transducers. However, at the present time lasers are much more expensive and much less reliable than LEDs. Although they are not currently widely used in LAN applications, we can expect them to be used almost universally in the foreseeable future as the price comes down and the reliability increases to make them relatively competitive with the LED. We can then expect LANs to be handling data rates of 100 Gbits/s or more with several digital video channels being handled by the same fibre network link.

8
The Integrated Services Digital
Network

INTRODUCTION.

The conversion to digital transmission and switching of speech signals in the public telephone network is proceeding at such a rate that it is likely to be almost universal within the next decade or so.   The only part of the network which has not to date seen much of a significant move towards the use of digital techniques for the transmission of speech is the local connections between the user and the local exchange. However, with the rapid progress of technology towards a greater use of large-scale integration of circuits onto a single chip, it is now becoming a practical proposition to provide analogue-to-digital and digital-to-analogue conversion in each telephone handset.   Work is therefore progressing towards providing digital transmission over the user's line.   The result of this will be that high-speed digital transmission facilities will be available from user's apparatus to user's apparatus.   It then becomes unnecessary to distinguish between speech and data signals, the same network being available for both without discrimination.   This has led to the concept of an Integrated Services Digital Network (ISDN).

Standards for operation of an ISDN, including network signalling and network interfacing, have now been produced by CCITT in the "I" series of recommendations.   These recommendations are based on the OSI seven-layer model concept.   We shall review these recommendations in this final chapter and take a quick look at how the ISDN is likely to evolve in the not-too-distant future. Already very much higher bit-rates than are presently being introduced are being proposed for the future, based on the use of optical fibres as the transmission medium.   The bit-rates envisaged will enable the network to be used for a number of new services, including digitally-encoded video signals for use in connection with video-phone and similar applications.   However, we must concern ourselves here first with the current proposals for an ISDN which we can expect to be implemented widely within the immediate future.

BASIS FOR ISDN

A network providing digital transmission and switching of telephony between local exchanges based on 64 kbits/s channels is commonly referred to as an Integrated Digital Network (IDN).   The conversion of an IDN into an ISDN involves digitisation of the local loop and the provision of a signalling system between the user and the IDN.   These processes are usually referred to as Digital Access.   The relationship between ISDN, IDN and Digital Access is illustrated in Fig.8.1.

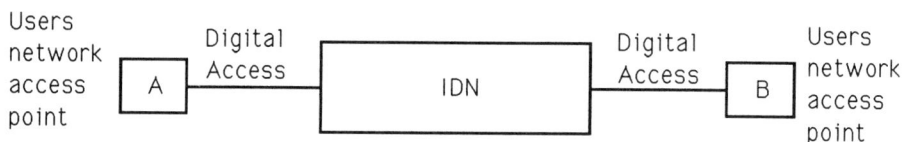

Fig.8.1 - ISDN as the combination of IDN and Digital Access.

DIGITAL ACCESS

Various proposals for digital access signalling rates over local lines have been made. The standard that has now emerged provides a basic data throughput rate of 144 kbits/s full-duplex.   The 144 kbits/s will actually appear to the user as three separate channels, two at 64 kbits/s and one at 16 kbits/s.   The 16 kbits/s is reserved for signalling purposes and is designated the 'D' channel.   The two independent 64 kbits/s channels are for use either for the conveyance of data or for PCM encoded voice signals and are designated 'B' channels.   The B channels are transparent to the user data and are switched by the network to provide an end-to-end transmission service.   A B channel path is established by signalling messages in the D channel. The D channel carries the signalling information using a layer 2 link access protocol known as LAP D.   The LAP D format is based on HDLC, which was described earlier in chapter 6.   However, additional addressing is provided so that up to 8 user terminals can operate through a single user network access point.

Two techniques are currently used to obtain full-duplex operation over the local line.   The first is known as 'burst-mode' or 'ping-pong' operation.   In this technique, short bursts of data are sent alternately from each end of the communication path.

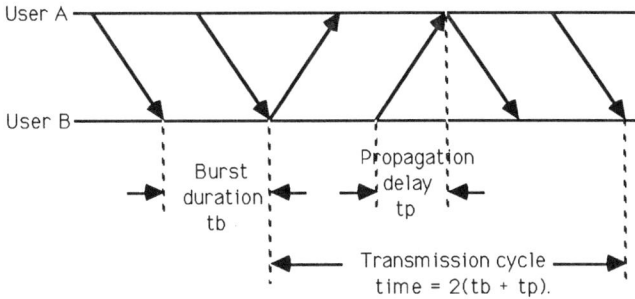

Fig.8.2 - Burst-mode timing diagram.

Fig.8.2 shows the timing of bursts in each direction.   If each user waits until he has received a burst from the other user before he proceeds to transmit his own burst of data, then the overall time for one cycle of transmission (i.e. the time for the transmission of one complete burst in each direction) is equal to the sum of the two burst durations and twice the propagation delay through the channel.   A possible choice of packet size that we might use as a suitable basis for a single burst in transmission is 36 bits.   This would consist of 16 bits (2 octets) for each of the B channels and 4 bits for the D channel.   This choice is based on a packet structure recommended by CCITT for another purpose, to be discussed later.   To achieve a throughput rate of 144 kbits/s, the transmission cycle time for 36 bits must be equal to 250 μS.   If the propagation delay were of the order of 50μS, then, to transmit two bursts of 36 bits in each direction in each transmission cycle, a basic transmission rate of the order of 500 kbits/s is necessary.   Originally it was expected that only one B channel and one D channel would be provided, and this could easily have been achieved over most local lines using burst-mode operation. However, the likelyhood of achieving a basic transmission rate of 500 kbits/s over a significant proportion of existing local lines, at least in the UK, is very dubious. This method is therefore now loosing favour with most telecommunication network operators, although it is still being proposed for use by some operators at the present time. Since the CCITT recommendations are only concerned with the data format at the user side of the line terminating unit and do not recommend any specific method of achieving transmission over the actual local line, the method of transmission over the line is a matter of choice for the individual network operator.

The second method is the use of electronic hybrid circuits where transmission in each direction takes place simultaneously but the signal being transmitted by a given terminal is subtracted from that being received from the line by the same terminal, so leaving only the signal from the other terminal at the receiver input. This means that the basic transmission rate is equal to the single direction data throughput rate, rather less than half that required for burst-mode. In fact the 2B1Q code, described earlier in Chapter 3, is being used by BT for integrated digital access in the UK, giving a further 50% reduction in the line signalling rate. This, in turn, gives a 50% reduction in bandwidth requirement. A schematic diagram of the electronic hybrid arrangement is given in Fig.8.3.

The proper operation of the hybrid depends on a good match in the balancing network between the line impedance and the balancing impedance. This is difficult to achieve in practice because climatic and other conditions will affect the line impedance in such a way that it is difficult to compensate for these changes. It is therefore necessary to provide further compensation in the form of an adaptive electronic echo-cancellor. This operates in the same way as the adaptive equaliser

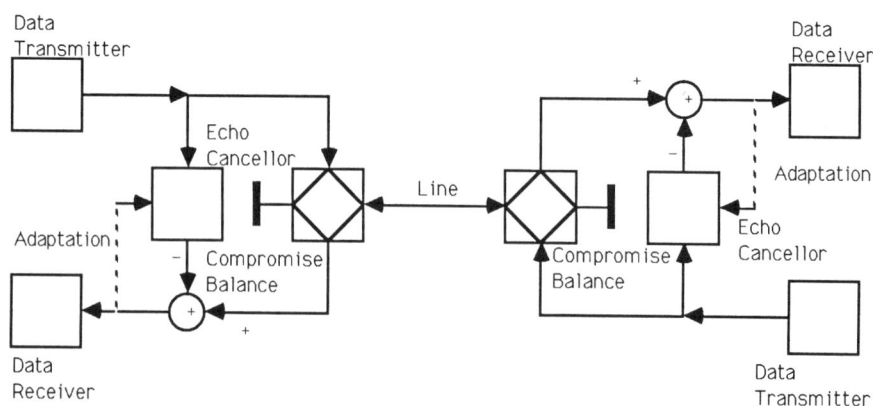

Fig.8.3 - Hybrid balance multiplex system (with echo cancellation).

described in chapter 1, except that in this case the cancelling signal is derived from the sender output rather than the signal at the receiver input.

THE USER INTERFACE

In CCITT terminology, the users network access point is referred to as the Network Termination (NT). The CCITT Network Terminating Unit Type 1 (NT1) allows up to 8 terminals to share the use of a single 2B + D 144 kbits/s digital access facility. CCITT recommendation I420 specifies the interface between the terminal equipment and the NT1. It uses a passive bus strategy which can provide multiple access as shown in Fig.8.4.

The socket in the NT1 is the end of the ISDN and the beginning of the users domain. The four-wire passive bus is plugged directly into this socket. The bus can operate in either of two modes, point-to-point or point-to-multipoint. In the point-to-point mode one Terminal Equipment (TE) is connected at the end of up to about 1 km of cable. In the point-to-multipoint mode up to 8 terminals can be connected in parallel anywhere along the bus, but the bus length is now limited to 200 metres. Over this bus passes the data for the two B channels and the D channel, plus some other bits which are used for miscellaneous purposes such as frame

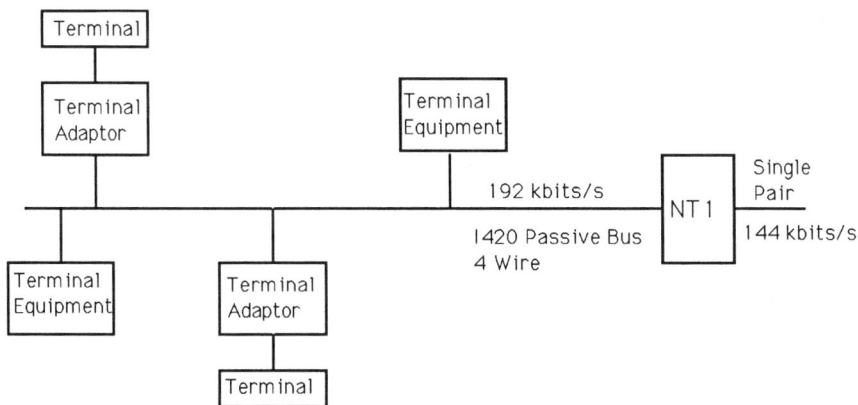

Up to 8 Terminal Equipments or Apaptors can be supported on a Basic Rate Access Passive Bus.

Fig.8.4 - I420 terminal configurations

synchronisation.   The B channels contain the user data which is switched by the network to provide end-to-end transmission service.   A B channel path is established by signalling messages in the D channel.   In a multi-terminal situation, all terminals have access to the D channel by the use of an access procedure but each B channel is allocated to a particular terminal during call set-up and is not capable of being shared between terminals.

OSI layer 1 service is realised using a two-pair cable that must be capable of supporting transmission at 192 kbits/s.   Transmission is based on a frame structure of 48 bits, 36 of these bits being 2 octets for each of the B channels and 4 bits for the D channel.   The other 12 bits are used for frame synchronisation and code balance purposes.   The line code used is Alternate Mark Inversion (AMI), a logical 1 being transmitted as a space and a logical 0 as a mark.   The frame structure is given in Fig.8.5.   It will be seen that there is a two bit off-set between the transmit and

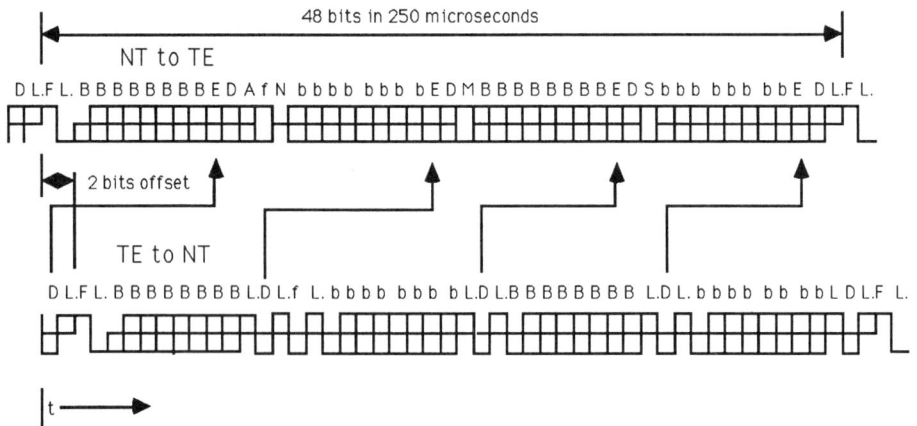

F = framing bit
L = DC balancing bit
D = D channel bit
E = D echo-channel bit
f = auxiliary framing bit

N = bit set to ternary value 'space'
B = bit within B1 channel
b = bit within B2 channel
A = bit used for activation
S = reserved for future standardisation
M = multiframing bit

Notes:
a) Dots demarcate those parts of the frame that are independently DC-balanced.
b) The f bit in the direction TE to NT is used as a Q bit if the Q channel capability is required.
c) The nominal 2 bit offset is as seen from the TE. The corresponding offset at the NT may be greater due to delay in the interface cable and varies by configuration.

Fig.8.5 - I420 layer 1 frame structure.

receive frames, this being the delay between a frame start at the receiver of a terminal and the frame start of the transmitted signal. A 10 bit off-set is also shown between the D channel leaving a teminal, travelling to the NT and being echoed back in the E channel. This 10 bit delay is made up of bus and transmission delays in the NT. A frame contains several L bits. These are balancing bits to prevent a build up of DC on the line. The frames are split into balanced blocks as represented by dots on the diagram. For the direction TE to NT, where each B channel may come from a different terminal, each terminal's output contains an L bit to form a balanced block.

Examining the frame in the NT to TE direction, the first bits in the frame are the F/L pair, which is used in the frame alignment procedure. The start of a new frame is signalled by the F/L pair violating the AMI rule. Obviously, once a violation has occurred, to restore correct polarity before the next frame there must be a second violation. This occurs with the first mark after the F/L pair. The f bit ensures this second violation occurs should there not be a mark in the B1, B2 D, E or A channels. The A bit is used in the activation procedure to indicate to the terminals that the system is in synchronisation. Next is an octet from the B2 channel, a bit of the E channel and a bit of the D channel, followed by an M bit. This is provided for multiframing purposes where applicable. The B1, B2, D and E channels are then repeated along with the S bit, which is a spare bit.

A D channel contention access procedure is used that ensures that, even when two or more terminals attempt to access the D channel simultaneously, one terminal will always be able to successfully complete the transmission of information. This procedure relies on the fact that the information to be transmitted consists of layer 2 HDLC type frames which are delimited by flags consisting of the binary pattern 01111110 and that zero bit insertion (bit-stuffing) is used to prevent flag imitation in the data. The interframe time fill consists of binary 1s which are represented by ternary space. A space is represented by zero line signal, which is generated by the TE transmitter going high impedance. This means a binary 0 from a parallel terminal will overwrite a binary 1. Detection of a collision is effected by the terminal monitoring the E channel (the D channel echoed from the NT). To access the D channel a terminal looks for the interframe time fill by counting the number of consecutive binary 1s in the D channel. Should a binary 0 be received, the count is reset. When the number of consecutive 1s reaches a predetermined value greater than the number of consecutive 1s possible in a frame because of the zero bit insertion algorithm, the counter is reset and the terminal may access the D channel.

When a terminal has just completed transmitting a frame the value of the count needed to be reached before another frame may be transmitted is incremented by 1. This gives other terminals a chance to access the channel. Hence an access and priority mechanism is established. There is still the possibility of a collision between two terminals of the same priority. This is detected and resolved by each terminal comparing its last transmitted bit with the next E bit. If they are the same the terminal continues to transmit. If, however, they are different, the terminal detecting the difference ceases transmission immediately and returns to the D channel monitoring state, leaving the other terminal to continue transmission.

The B channels simply provide a transparent transmission facility at 64 kbits/s and therefore require no higher layers of protocol. The network control function is provided by the D channel. The layer 2 link access procedure for the D channel is referred to as LAP D. LAP D is based on HDLC and is therefore similar to the LAP B procedure used with X25 and described in Chapter 6. The most significant difference is the use of frame multiplexing at layer 2 allowing several LAPs to exist on the same physical connection. It is this feature that allows up to 8 terminals to share the signalling channel in the passive bus arrangement shown in Fig.8.4. Multiplexing is achieved by using a separate address for each LAP in the system. To carry the LAP identity an address field of two octets in length is used. This identifies the receiver of a command frame and the transmitter of a response frame. It has only local significance and is used only by the two communicating end points to identify the LAP. It is not used by the network for routing purposes. Addresses for routing are contained in the layer 3 information field. The LAP frame structure is given in Fig.8.6.

The address field is divided into two parts. The first octet is known as the Service Access Point Identifier (SAPI) and is used to identify the service for which the signalling frame is intended. This gives the network the option of handling signalling associated with different services such as telephony and packet-switched data. The second octet is the Terminal Endpoint Identifier (TEI). This is used to identify the particular terminal involved on the passive bus connected to the NT1,

Octet 1	0	1	1	1	1	1	1	0	Opening flag

Octet 2 — Address octet 1
Octet 3 — Address octet 2
Octet 4 — Control octet 1
Octet 5 — Control octet 2 *
Octet 6 — Layer 3 information

The structure of the control field depends on the frame type (See Fig.8.7).

Octet n-3

Octet n-2 — FCS octet 1 — Frame check sequence
Octet n-1 — FCS octet 2 — Frame check sequence

Octet n	0	1	1	1	1	1	1	0	Closing flag

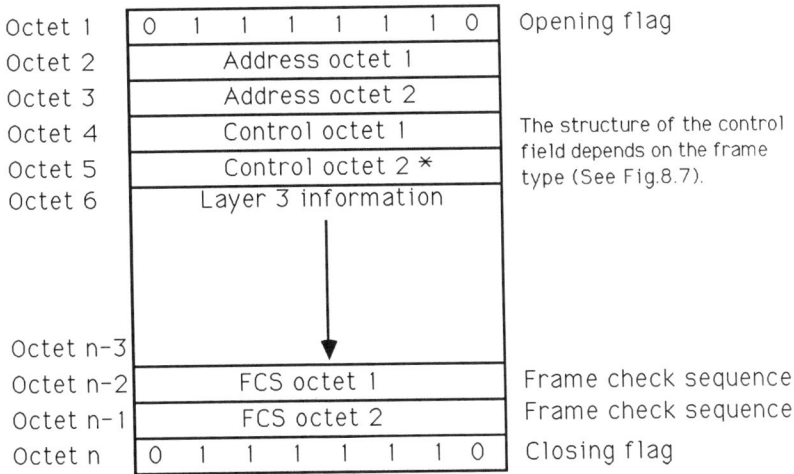

* The second octet of the control field is not always present,

Fig.8.6 - I420 Layer 2 (LAP D) frame structure

each terminal being associated with a unique TEI value. The combination of SAPI and TEI identify the LAP and provide a unique layer 2 address.

The remainder of the frame is similar to LAP B, except that two octets are used in the control field in Information and Supervisory frames because 7 bits are used for the sequence numbers N(S) and N(R) instead of the three used in LAP B. The control field formats are given in Fig.8.7.

The function of LAP D is to deliver layer 3 frames across a layer 1 interface, as far as possible error-free and in sequence. Error control and sequencing are caried out as for LAP B. Layer 3 provides digital-access signalling on a common signalling channel basis. At the time of writing, there is no definitive standard for a layer 3 protocol. The BT pilot ISDN used a system known as Digital Access Signalling System No.1 (DASS1), but this was based on a 8 kbits/s, rather than a 16 kbits/s, signalling facility. The purpose of the signalling system is to allow the user to instruct the network of his requirements to enable the network to be configured to provide for this service. The layer 3 control and address information is transmitted using International Alphabet No.5 (IA5) characters.

(a) Information Frame	0	N(S)		Octet 4
	P/F	N(R)		Octet 5

(b) Supervisory Frame	1	0	S	X		Octet 4
	P/F			N(R)		Octet 5

(c) Unnumbered Frame	1	1	M	P/F	M		Octet 4

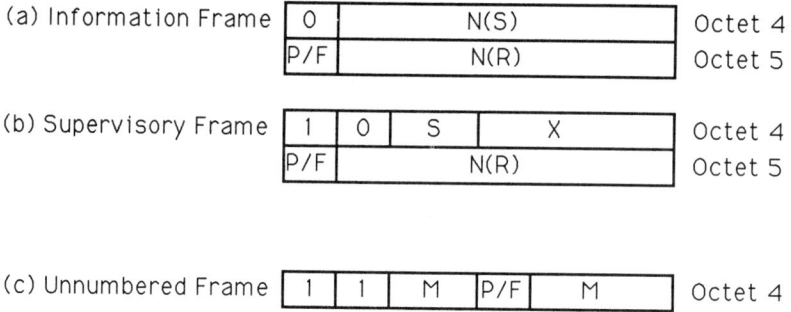

N(S) = Transmitter send sequence number
N(R) = Transmitter receive sequence number
S   = Supervisory function bits
M   = Modifier function bits
P/F = Poll/Final bit.
X   = Reserved bits, normally set to 0

Fig.8.7 - I420 Layer 2 (LAP D) Control field formats.

PRIMARY RATE ACCESS

At the local exchange, the B channels are multiplexed for onward transmission into the 30 x 64 kbits/s group transmission facility already associated with 30 channel PCM. Associated with each 30 channel group are two further 64 kbits/s channels, one is used for network and frame synchronisation and the other for signalling. This gives a total transmission rate of 32 x 64 kbits/s = 2 .048 Mbits/s. This 2.048 Mbits/s facility is referred to as primary rate access. The 2.048 Mbits/s stream is divided into frames of 256 bits. The 32 channels are time-division-multiplexed into 32 slots each containing 8 bits from the appropriate channel to form the 256 bit frame as shown in Fig.8.8. Slot 0 is used to transmit timing and frame

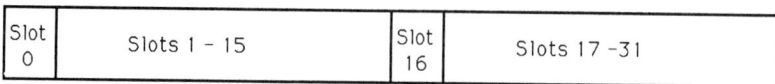

Slot 0	Slots 1 - 15	Slot 16	Slots 17 -31

Fig.8.8 - Primary rate access frame structure

synchronisation information, slots 1 to 15 and 17 to 31 each carry 8 bits for each of the 30 information channels and slot 16 carries the signalling information. The primary rate access thus provides inter-exchange communication as shown in Fig.8.9. The D channel signalling associated with 30 B channels is statistically

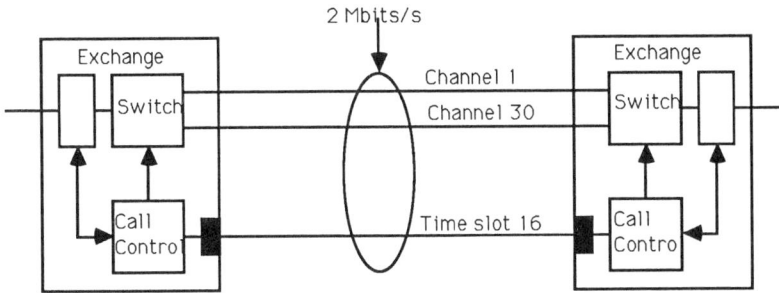

Fig.8.9 - Primary rate access interconnected exchanges.

multiplexed onto the 64 kbits/s signalling channel in time slot 16 using Digital Access Signalling System No.2 (DASS2). This is usually referred to as common channel signalling, as the signalling associated with all the channels is carried together in one single signalling channel. The basis for common channel signalling is the CCITT signalling system No.7. The common channel signalling is message-based, each message carrying information indicating to which traffic channel it refers. Messages from different traffic channels are interleaved to share the transmission facility. The details of the operation of the common channel signalling is beyond the scope of this book and, in any case, is not usually of interest to the network user. Its operation is exclusively the concern of the network service provider.

SUPPLEMENTARY SERVICES

The DASS2 signalling system is able to support a number of supplementary services as follows:

a) Closed User Group (CUG).

The network facilitates the establishment of a closed community of users so that calls between members of the same CUG are allowed, whilst communication with non-members of the CUG is generally inhibited. A typical closed user group arrangement is illustrated in Fig.8.10.

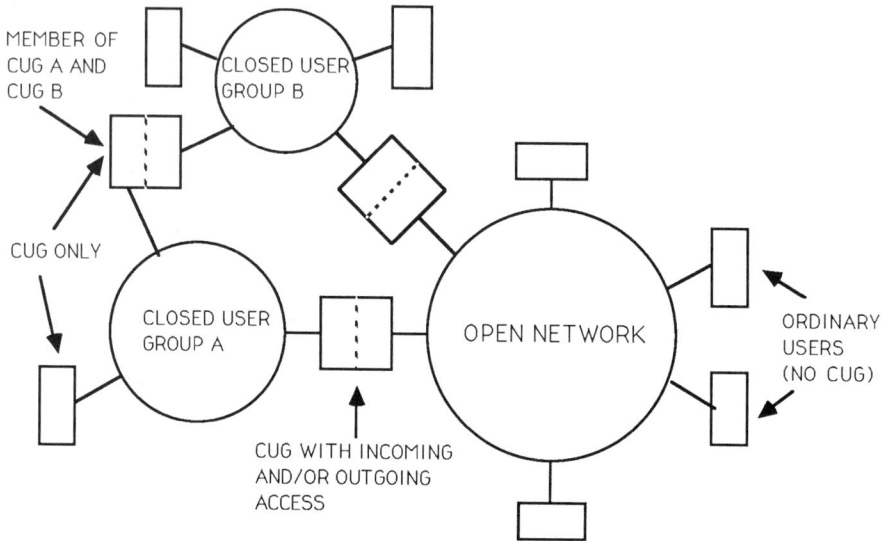

Fig.8.10 - Closed user group configuration.

b) Calling and Called Line Identity (CLI).

The network will provide a registered user of the service with the address of the remote call party during call establishment.

c) Network Address Extension.

This service provides the calling party with the possibility of including up to six International Alphabet No.5 (IA5) characters as an extension to the Called Party Number. These characters will be passed to the called user at the time of indicating the incoming call and may be used to direct the call to the appropriate end-point within the called customer's equipment.

d) Call Charge Indication.

This service provides an indication of the call charge at the end of the call.

e) User-to-User Signalling.

This service supports the conveyance of blocks of signalling information transparently through the network, between the two parties of a call. Each information block may be up to 32 octets in length. The network places no restrictions on the coding of this information other than requiring each block to contain an integral number of octets.

THE FUTURE BROADBAND ISDN

As optical fibres penetrate more and more into the telecommunications network, it is envisaged that a broadband ISDN (B-ISDN) will be provided in the not-too-distant future. This will have the advantage of providing facilities for high-speed digital applications such as digital video. Already some trial B-ISDNs are in operation in Europe and the USA and it is expected that some standards will soon emerge. Rates that have been proposed are:

H1 - 2 Mbits/s (Primary Access Rate).

H2 - 30 to 45 Mbits/s.

H3 - 60 to 70 Mbits/s.

H4 - 120 to 140 Mbits/s.

These rates are based on requirements for digital video services. It is likely that network interface rates of 150 Mbits/s and probably 600 Mbits/s, will be provided. In terms of channels, the interface structure will be of the form pH4 + qH3 + rH2 + sH1 + mB + D, where p, q, r, s and m are integers.

The study and development of broadband services is being co-ordinated under the RACE (Research in Advanced Communications for Europe) programme. The RACE programme is targetted towards the provision of widely available broad-band ISDN services by 1995. There is thus an exciting future for the development of data services towards the 21st Century.

Bibliography

Beauchamp, K. G. (1987) *Computer communications*. Van Nostrand Reinhold.

Bennett, W. R. and Davey, J. R. (1965) *Data transmission*. McGraw-Hill.

Brewster, R. L. (1986) *Telecommunications technology*. Ellis Horwood.

Brewster, R. L. (ed.), (1986) *Data communications and networks*. Peter Peregrinus.

Bylanski, P. and Ingram, D. G. W. (1976) *Digital tranmission systems*. Peter Peregrinus.

Cheong, A. B. and Hirschheim, R. A. (1983) *Local area networks*. John Wiley.

Clark, A. P. (1976) *Principles of digital data transmission*. Pentech.

Davies, D. W. and Barber, D. L. A. (1973) *Communication networks for computers*. John Wiley.

Deasington, R. (1984) *A practical guide to computer communications and networking*. 2nd edn. Ellis Horwood.

Deasington, R. (1985) *X25 explained*. Ellis Horwood.

Griffiths, J. M. (ed.), (1988) *Local telecommunications 2 - into the digital era* . 2nd edn. Peter Peregrinus.

Hagelbarger, D. W. (1959) *Recurrent codes: easily mechanised, burst-correcting binary codes*. BSTJ. **38**, 969-984.

Halsall, F. (1988) *Data communications, computer networks and OSI*. 2nd edn. Addison Wesley.

Hamming, R. W. (1980) *Coding and information theory*. Prentice-Hall.

Haykin, S. (1988) *Digital communications*.Wiley.

Jesty, P. H. (1985) *Networking with microcomputers*. Blackwell.

Kretzmer, E. R. (1976) *Generalisation of a technique for binary data communications*. IEEE Trans. Comm., **14**, 67-68.

Lucky, R. W., Salz, J. and Weldon, E. J. (1968) *Principles of data transmission.* McGraw-Hill.

Marshall, G. J. (1980) *Principles of digital communications,* McGraw-Hill.

National Computing Centre (1982) *Handbook of data communications.*

Nyquist, H. (1928) *Certain topics in telegraph transmission theory.* Trans. AIEE, **47**, 617-644.

Purser, M. (1987) *Computers and telecommunications networks.* Blackwell.

Ronayne, J. (1987) *The integrated Servies digital network; from conception to application.* Pitman.

Savage, J. E. (1967) *Some simple self-synchronizing digital data scramblers.* BSTJ. **46**, 449-487.

Shannon, C. E. (1948) *A mathematical theory of communication.* BSTJ. **27**, 379-423 and 623-656.

Sherman, K. (1981) *Data communications, a user's guide.* Reston.

Stallings, W. (1984) *Local networks.* Collier-Macmillan.

Wade, J. G. (1987) *Signal coding and processing.* Ellis Horwood.

Tutorial Questions

QUESTIONS: CHAPTER 1

1.1 What features determine the fundamental limit to the rate at which data can be transmitted over a communication channel? What are the necessary criteria to achieve in practice a transmission rate approaching the theoretical maximum?

1.2 What is an 'eye-pattern' and why is it useful in assessing the quality of a data transmission channel?

1.3 Why is equalisation sometimes necessary on a base-band data transmission channel? Discuss techniques for the implementation of automatic pre-set and adaptive equalisers.

QUESTIONS: CHAPTER 2

2.1 The public telephone network is widely used for data transmission despite the fact it is not designed to carry digital signals. Explain why this is so. List the shortcomings of the network for data communication and explain how these shortcomings are overcome in practice.

2.2 Explain why modems are necessary to enable data signals to be sent over the public switched telephone network (PSTN). Describe the principle of operation of an f.s.k. modem suitable for 200 bits/s full-duplex transmission over the PSTN. Why is this method of modulation unsuitable for high-speed data applications?

2.3 Describe the principles of operation of a phase-shift-keyed (psk) modem suitable for 2400 bits/s half-duplex transmission over the PSTN. Why is differential phase-shift-keying (dpsk) used in practice rather than basic psk? What, if any, are the disadvantages of dpsk?

QUESTIONS: CHAPTER 3

3.1 Explain why line codes are often used in connection with the transmission of digital data. List and describe the desirable features of a line code. Show in which ways and to what extent the WAL 1 (Manchester) code meets these requirements.

3.2 Line codes are often employed in the transmission of data over digital communication networks. State: a) Why line codes are necessary. b) The desirable features of a line code. Give two examples of practical line codes and explain their salient features.

QUESTIONS: CHAPTER 4

4.1 Explain the concept of 'Forward Error Correction' in data transmission and say how this differs from correction by retransmission (ARQ). Describe how a simple Hamming Code can be used to correct single errors per block of data. What happens when two bits are in error in a single block?

4.2 In many practical data transmission systems, transmission errors are likely to occur in short bursts. Describe an error-correcting code that is designed to correct short bursts of errors. State any limitations in the effectiveness of such a code and describe any trade-off that can be achieved in the code design.

QUESTIONS: CHAPTER 5

5.1 Briefly define the function of each of the layers in the OSI seven layer model for Open Systems Interconnection. Show how the first three layers are embedded in the CCITT recommendation X25 protocol for packet switching networks. Explain briefly the function of the Frame Check Sequence used in the X25 format.

5.2 Describe briefly the concept of polling in a data communication network. Highlight the differences between roll-call polling and hub polling and state the factors which would influence your choice of polling strategy.

5.3 What do you understand by the term 'multiplexor'? Why are multiplexors used in long-distance data communication?   What are the special features of a 'statistical multiplexor' and what are its advantages and disadvantages compared with the conventional multiplexor?

QUESTIONS: CHAPTER 6

6.1 Describe the basic operation of a packet-switched network. Why is it necessary to number in sequence consecutive packets forming a single message? What impact does this have on the use of packet-switched networks for the transmission of digitally-encoded speech?

6.2 Describe the basic features of the X25 network access protocol and show how it corresponds to the first three levels of the I S O seven layer model for open systems interconnection.

6.3 Give brief details of the main features of the H D L C link level protocol. Describe how HDLC packets are delimited by the use of flags and explain what steps are taken to ensure that the flag sequence is not duplicated within the data field. Show how the frame check sequence (FCS) is used to detect errors in the data field. Comment on the limit to the power of the FCS to detect multiple errors in the field. What are the main uses of the H D L C protocol?

6.4 Explain the difference in operation between a packet-switched and a circuit-switched data network. What are the relative merits of the two types of network? How can intercommunication between the two types of network be achieved? Describe briefly any apparatus needed to make the interconnection.

QUESTIONS: CHAPTER 7

7.1 Compare briefly the 'Ring' and 'Bus' configurations used in Local Area Networks. In particular, discuss the differing techniques required to access both types of network. Give examples to illustrate the difference between the strategies employed in each case.

7.2 Describe the operation of 'empty-slot' and 'token-passing' as access control strategies for ring configured local area networks. State the factors which would influence your choice of strategy.

7.3 Describe the operation of the 'Cambridge Ring' local area network strategy. Explain in some detail the precautions taken to prevent packets circulating indefinitely in the network, thus preventing other users gaining access.

7.4 Describe the operation of a bus configured local area network employing the 'Ethernet' strategy. Explain how the 'carrier sense multiple access with collision detection' (CSMA/CD) strategy operates and state what precautions have to be taken to prevent repeated collisions on successive attempts at simultaneous call initiation.

QUESTIONS: CHAPTER 8

8.1 Describe the basic features of an integrated services digital network (ISDN). Discuss in some detail the requirements for Digital Access to enable individual ISDN users to obtain access to the main integrated digital network (IDN).

8.2 List some of the enhanced services that become possible with the introduction of ISDN and discuss their usefulness to communications network users.

Index